THE COMPLETE
PARTY
COOKBOOK

THE COMPLETE
PARTY
COOKBOOK

Compiled by Coral Walker

a Salamander book

Published by Salamander Books Limited
LONDON • NEW YORK

A SALAMANDER BOOK

Published by Salamander Books Ltd.,
129/137 York Way,
London N7 9LG,
United Kingdom.

This edition © Salamander Books Ltd. 1990

ISBN 0 86101 501 0

Distributed by Hodder and Stoughton Services,
PO Box 6, Mill Road, Dunton Green,
Sevenoaks, Kent TN13 2XX

CREDITS

Introductions written by: Coral Walker

Editors: Lisa Dyer and Coral Walker

Contributing authors: Pat Alburey, June Budgen, Sarah Bush,
Linda Fraser, Annette Grimsdale, Kerenza Harries,
Lesley Mackley, Janice Murfitt, Cecilia Norman, Lorna Rhodes,
Jenny Ridgwell, Louise Steele, Sally Taylor, Steven Wheeler

Designer: Rachael Stone

Typeset: Angel Graphics Ltd.

Filmset: SX Composing Ltd.

Colour separation: Fotographics Ltd.,
J. Film Process Ltd., Kentscan Limited,
Magnum Graphics Limited, New Interlitho S.p.A.

Photographers: Per Ericson, Paul Grater,
Sue Jorgensen, Ray Joyce, Alan Newnham,
John Stewart, Alister Thorpe

Printed in Italy

CONTENTS

AN INTRODUCTION TO PARTY-GIVING

Most people enjoy attending a party but not everyone welcomes the idea of entertaining. Even the most experienced cook can be overwhelmed at the prospect of catering for a dozen ten year-olds or twenty wedding guests.

In this book we have endeavoured to make party-giving and cooking as much fun and as little problem as possible. We have included recipes that will give new inspiration to the experienced chef as well as ideas and tips for the novice. For easy reference, this book is divided into six chapters. These chapters are based on different party occasions: buffets, barbecues, cocktail parties, dinner parties, children's parties and seasonal parties which cover annual events such as Christmas and Halloween.

Each chapter opens with a general introduction to the specific party, giving suggestions to help you prepare for the event, from setting up your room or table to organising entertainment. Each chapter contains a large selection of colourfully-illustrated and mouth-watering recipes to serve.

The selection of recipes offers a total approach, from the appetizer to the dessert. Also included are drinks to accompany the food and to suit the type of party. All the recipes were chosen not only to complement each other for their taste and appearance, but also for their nutritional value. In most cases we have steered away from the obvious and have instead provided interesting and unusual variations on more standard fare.

To create your own unique party and imbue it with your personal style, consider the suggestions on the following pages regarding preparation and atmosphere. Also, cross-reference the recipes throughout this book and invent your own combination of tastes.

PARTY PREPARATION

Any party will run a lot more smoothly with a little forward-planning. The more preparation you do, the less unforseen circumstances arise, and the less you will panic. Above all, you want to avoid being unprepared when your guests arrive.

Menu Planning Plan a meal at least a fortnight in advance. Choose a range of dishes for your menu which complement each other visually and in taste and texture. Do not have all soft foods, or all crispy dishes. Also, avoid too many of the same colours or shapes. Serve dishes in a variety of ways but avoid too many small pieces. If you are serving one vegetable puréed, ensure another one is chopped or whole.

You may want to experiment with an unfamiliar recipe before the day of the party. Use the previous week to work out the amounts for subtle flavourings or spicing as well as any imperfections and timing problems.

Shop for all non-perishable ingredients two weeks in advance. Use a detailed shopping list, organised by the layout of your local supermarket. If your supermarket does not stock some of the items you need, make sure an alternative shop does stock it regularly. Buy plenty of the ingredients; you do not want to run short of any items at the last minute.

Tables & Tableware About a week in advance, check that you have ample crockery, cutlery and glassware as well as table linen (see page 52). All these items should be clean and polished. If you are holding a children's party, it is advisable to buy paper plates and bowls. There are excellent ranges of children's partyware bearing brightly coloured cartoon characters available from most stationery suppliers.

At this time, it is also worth checking that you have enough seating and a large enough table. If necessary, borrow from friends or neighbours. Or, if you are holding a large party such as a buffet, you may want to hire banquet tables and chairs from an outside company.

Setting & Atmosphere A beautiful table setting and a pleasant atmosphere can set the tone for the party. But do not overdo it. Your table is meant to be a pleasing background for the food so it does not have to be overwhelming or extravagant. Remember that the most lovely things are often the most simple. Try not to put too much on the table or your guests will not have room to eat. If you find the table becoming overburdened, by all means dispense with the decorations.

A table without a tablecloth will certainly need a central display. For dinner parties, keep the display low; guests will not appreciate craning their necks around long-stemmed flowers to talk to each other.

Candles are frequently used for table settings, and they add a soft and intimate light to the occasion. Buy co-ordinating candles and do not forget to make sure that they fit the candle holders you plan to use. If the candles do not fit securely, they may easily topple over and empty hot wax on to your tablecloth, or worse, on to someone's clothes.

Pleasant sounds and aromas are strong mood-setters. Do have soft music playing in the background to enhance the atmosphere of the party but be sure your music suits the occasion. You will probably have no trouble providing inviting and mouth-watering smells for your guests.

TIME-SAVING TIPS

During your week of preparation, think about ways to save time on the day of the party. This could prove invaluable if anything unexpected occurs.

Many dishes, such as desserts or appetizers, can be prepared in advance, either frozen, refrigerated or kept in airtight containers. If your recipe is dough-based, a supply of dough or pastry can be kept frozen in your freezer for when you need it.

Some leaf and all root vegetables can be washed, although not necessarily peeled, in advance and refrigerated. However, do not wash lettuce too far in advance; the leaves will wilt and sometimes discolour.

Shredded cheese, boiled eggs, chopped herbs (we recommend using fresh herbs whenever possible), salad dressings, relishes, some sauces and spice mixtures such as garam masala and tandoori masala (see page 13) can all be prepared several days before your party.

Garnishes and decorations can be prepared in advance and refrigerated in plastic bags or airtight boxes. Make citrus butterflies or other cocktail shapes, wash parsley, chop nuts and stone olives or cherries.

For buffets, cocktail parties and children's parties, cook dishes in disposable aluminium dishes to avoid extra washing up. Remember, never use aluminium in a microwave oven.

HOSPITALITY

Hospitality is perhaps the most essential key to a party's success. All the effort taken over the room, atmosphere, table setting and food is of no use if visitors are more or less left to their own devices. You do not want to be so busy perfecting a complicated dish that you unwittingly ignore your guests. Make sure they are comfortable and relaxed and that they are offered refreshment on arrival.

Guests will be attending your party for good company and conversation as well as food and drink. Introduce them to the other guests and try to find some common ground they can discuss when you move on. Your visitors may forget what they were served to eat at your party but they will never forget you, so make a friendly and personable impression.

PORTION CONTROL

Guidelines when catering for large numbers of guests
(in approximate quantities per person)

Buffets
2-3 portions of main course
2 portions of vegetable dishes
1-2 portions of dessert
3-4 drinks or ½ bottle of wine

Barbecues
2-3 portions of main course
2-3 portions of vegetable dishes
1-2 portions of dessert
3-4 drinks

Cocktail Parties
5-6 small savoury snacks
4-5 drinks

Children's Parties
4-5 savoury snacks
1-2 sweet items or desserts
2 cold drinks

Drink Equivalents Per Bottle

Sherry, port, vermouth	12-16 glasses
Spirits	30 glasses (single measures)
Wine (70-75 cl)	5-6 glasses
Fruit cordial	20-25 drinks
Fruit juice (1 litre)	8-10 drinks

This colourful and stylish display of modern cutlery shows some of the possibilities available if you wish to colour-co-ordinate your china and cutlery. Traditional stainless steel, however, is much more versatile.

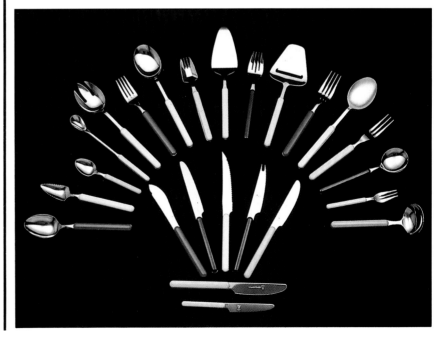

BUFFETS

Buffets are ideal for a large number of guests, whether the occasion is to celebrate an anniversary or a birthday. They are perfect for times when you need to offer something more substantial than a sandwich, but when there are too many people to provide a sit-down meal.

SMALL & LARGE PARTIES

Finding a suitable location for your buffet party depends on the number of guests you are inviting. With careful planning, about 40 people can be catered for in the home, but you may find that 20 to 30 is a more manageable number.

If you are planning to hold a larger buffet party, such as a wedding brunch, it will probably be necessary to hire a hall or marquee. A small marquee will fit into many average-sized gardens and it can be quite cost-effective. Also, unlike a rented hall, it allows close proximity to your own kitchen. Catering on this large scale will require additional help, so do secure the services of reliable friends or family. They can help you with setting up, preparing the food or simply greeting guests.

SETTING THE SCENE

Your buffet table will be the main attraction, so be sure it is eye-catching. This effect can be created with the menu you choose, as well as the table linen and decorations.

All plates, cutlery, food and drink should be well spaced on the table. One large table decoration in the centre and two or three smaller versions placed along the length of the table will provide an attractive overall effect. Beautiful cut flowers are one of the most simple decorations but they help make your table look like a work of art.

When you have a large number of people to serve, divide your dishes in two and arrange them symmetrically on the table. Guests can approach the table from both ends and meet in the middle. This will stop queues from forming at one end. If you are holding a wedding or anniversary buffet, remember to have a separate small table on which to place the cake.

FOOD & DRINK

In this chapter we have selected a range of delicious and colourful dishes that can be easily doubled or trebled to cater for larger numbers. All the recipes are designed to create a visual impact as well as a tasty one. Add to the effect by decorating and garnishing dishes lavishly, using cut fruit and vegetables or even orchid flowers.

You will want to concentrate your menu on several main course dishes and a smaller range of desserts. There is no need to offer appetizers, although small dishes such as Stuffed Eggs (see page 11) or a selection of dips (see pages 18-19) always proves popular. Plan for each guest taking three or four smaller portions of the main courses, two servings of salad or vegetable and between one to two desserts. Allow one to two aperitifs and a half bottle of wine per person. A good buffet will be tempting, and everyone will want to try several of the dishes you offer.

Pictured below, the buffet is shown in all its glory. The formality of an exquisite spread of food and drink with the informality of self-service makes a marvellous combination.

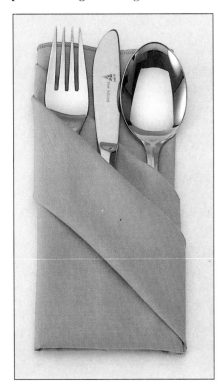

Above: Make a buffet napkin by folding a square in half twice. Take a layer from the corner and make three diagonal folds. Repeat with second layer, only narrower; tuck under first. Fold both sides back and insert cutlery.

COURGETTE PASTA MOULD

SPINACH CANNELLONI

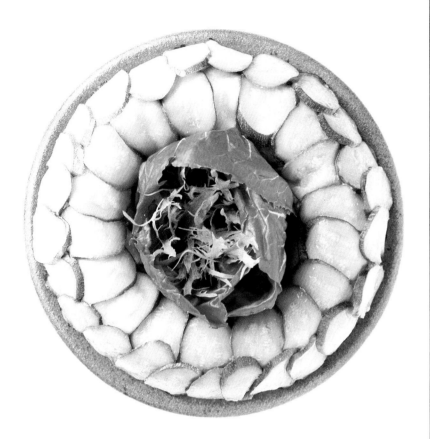

3 medium courgettes (zucchini), thinly sliced
125 g (4 oz/2¼ cups) wholewheat pasta wheat ears
6 teaspoons vegetable oil
1 large onion, finely chopped
4 tomatoes, peeled and chopped
3 teaspoons tomato purée (paste)
2 teaspoons chopped fresh oregano
1 egg, beaten
salt and pepper
30 g (1 oz/6 teaspoons) butter
radicchio and endive leaves, to serve

In a saucepan of boiling water, cook courgettes (zucchini) for 3-4 minutes until just tender. Drain, then rinse with cold water. Spread out on a tea towel.

In a large pan of boiling salted water, cook wheat ears until just tender. Drain. Meanwhile, heat oil in a frying pan. Add onion and cook gently until soft. In a bowl, mix together pasta, onion, tomatoes, tomato purée (paste), oregano and egg. Season to taste with salt and pepper.

Preheat oven to 200C (400F/Gas 6). Thoroughly butter a ring mould then line with courgette (zucchini) slices, overlapping them like tiles on a roof.

Fill mould with pasta mixture. Cover with overlapping courgette (zucchini) slices. Dot top with butter. Cover with foil. Bake in the oven for 40 minutes. Turn out onto a serving plate. Serve hot or cold with radicchio and endive leaves.

Serves 6.

500 g (1 lb) fresh spinach, trimmed and washed
30 g (1 oz/6 teaspoons) butter
1 onion, finely chopped
3 teaspoons plain flour
155 ml (5 fl oz/⅔ cup) milk
125 g (4 oz/½ cup) ham, finely chopped
salt and pepper
pinch of freshly grated nutmeg
8 ready-to-use cannelloni tubes
1 quantity Béchamel sauce, see below
90 g (3 oz/¾ cup) grated Cheddar cheese
slices of ham and bay leaves, to garnish

In a large saucepan, cook spinach in a little water until tender. Drain spinach and chop finely.

In a saucepan, melt butter, add onion and cook until soft. Stir in flour and cook for 1 minute. Gradually add milk and bring to the boil for 1 minute. Stir in spinach and ham. Season with salt, pepper and nutmeg. Push spinach mixture into cannelloni tubes.

Preheat oven to 220C (425F/Gas 7). In a saucepan, gently heat white sauce. Stir in 60 g (2 oz/½ cup) cheese. Pour half the sauce into an ovenproof dish. Arrange cannelloni in dish and pour over remaining sauce, arrange ham in a lattice pattern and sprinkle remaining cheese on top. Bake in the oven for 40 minutes until golden. Serve, garnished with bay leaves.

Serves 4.

BÉCHAMEL SAUCE

315 ml (10 fl oz/1¼ cups) milk
½ bay leaf
60 g (2 oz/6 teaspoons) butter
60 g (2 oz/½ cup) plain flour
salt and pepper

In a small saucepan, heat the milk and bay leaf to just below boiling point. Remove from heat. Remove bay leaf. In a heavy saucepan, melt butter. Stir in flour and cook for 2 minutes, stirring, over gentle heat. Remove from heat. Gradually stir in milk. Return pan to heat. Stir gently for 10 minutes. Season with salt and pepper.

SMOKED FISH MOUSSE

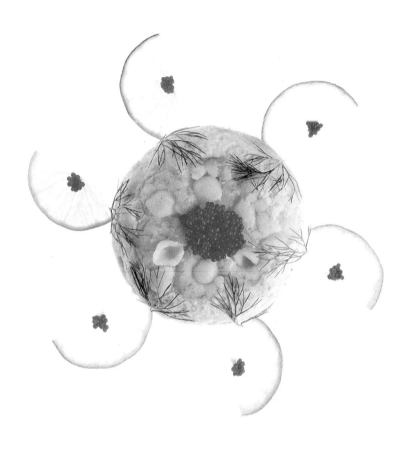

60 g (2 oz/1 cup) small pasta shells	
24 peeled prawns	
fennel leaves	
375 g (12 oz) smoked fish fillets, such as haddock, skinned and cut into pieces	
3 egg whites	
250 ml (8 fl oz/1 cup) double (thick) cream	
salt	
pinch of cayenne pepper	
lime slices, lumpfish roe and sprigs of dill, to garnish	

In a large saucepan of boiling salted water, cook pasta shells until tender. Drain.

Butter 6 individual ramekin dishes. Place 4 prawns and a piece of fennel in the bottom of each dish.

Preheat oven to 180C (350F/Gas 4). In a blender or food processor, process fish until smooth. Mix in egg whites and cream. Season with salt and cayenne pepper. Stir in pasta shells.

Divide mixture between ramekin dishes. Place dishes in a roasting tin. Pour in water to come halfway up dishes. Cook in the oven for about 15 minutes, or until firm. Turn out onto serving plates and garnish with lime slices, lumpfish roe and dill.

Serves 6.

DEVILLED CRAB QUICHE

250 g (8 oz/2 cups) plain flour	
½ teaspoon salt	
½ teaspoon chilli seasoning	
60 g (2 oz/¼ cup) block margarine, diced	
60 g (2 oz/¼ cup) lard, diced	
60 g (2 oz/¼ cup) finely grated Cheddar cheese	
6 rashers streaky bacon, chopped	
1 onion, chopped	
125 g (4 oz) crabmeat, flaked	
3 eggs	
155 ml (5 fl oz/⅔ cup) single (light) cream	
½ teaspoon dry mustard	
¼ teaspoon cayenne pepper	
tomato and sprig of parsley, to garnish	

Preheat oven to 200C (400F/Gas 6).

Put flour, salt and chilli seasoning into a bowl. Add margarine and lard and rub in finely until mixture resembles breadcrumbs. Add cheese and mix well. Stir in 3 tablespoons water and mix to form a firm dough. Knead gently. Roll out pastry and use to line a 25 cm (10 in) loose-bottomed, fluted flan tin, set on a baking sheet. Press pastry well into flutes and trim edge neatly. Prick base all over with a fork. Line flan with a piece of greaseproof paper and fill with baking beans.

Bake in the oven for 15 minutes, then remove paper and beans and return flan to oven for a further 5-10 minutes until dry and lightly golden. Meanwhile, dry-fry bacon in a pan for 3 minutes. Add onion and cook for 2 minutes. Remove from heat and mix with crabmeat. Spoon mixture into flan case. Whisk together eggs, cream, mustard and cayenne and season with salt. Pour into flan case. Bake for 30-35 minutes until golden. Serve, garnished with tomato and parsley.

Serves 6-8.

PRAWN BARQUETTES

STUFFED EGGS

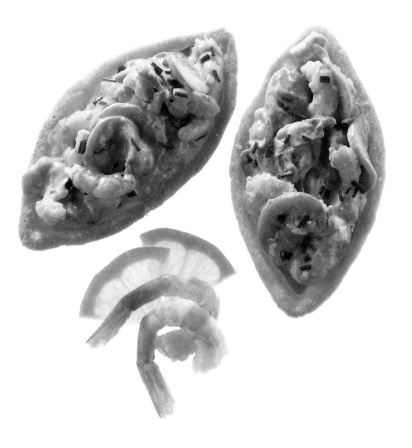

125 g (4 oz/1 cup) plain flour
pinch salt
3 teaspoons finely grated
Parmesan cheese
90 g (3 oz/⅓ cup) butter
1 egg yolk
prawns and lemon triangles, to garnish

FILLING:

45 g (1½ oz/9 teaspoons) butter
185 g (6 oz) button mushrooms, sliced
155 ml (5 fl oz/⅔ cup) thick sour cream
1-2 teaspoons dry sherry
90 g (3 oz) prawns, chopped
2-3 teaspoons fresh chopped chives

Put flour, salt, cheese and butter into a blender or food processor and process for 30 seconds. Add egg yolk and 4 teaspoons water and process until mixture binds together. Wrap in plastic wrap and leave to rest in the refrigerator for 20 minutes. Meanwhile, preheat the oven to 220C (425F/Gas 7).

Roll out pastry on a lightly floured surface until very thin. Lift pastry, using a rolling pin, and lay it over 12 barquette tins. Press down lightly and roll over tins to trim. Press pastry down in tins. Prick base of each tin and stack them one on top of each other 3 tins high. Top each stack with an empty tin.

Bake in the oven for 15 minutes. Remove from oven and unstack tins. Return single layer of tins to oven for 2-3 minutes to crisp. Leave to cool.

To make filling, melt butter in a pan and fry mushrooms for 1 minute. Pour in cream and bring to boil, stirring continuously until thickened. Add sherry, prawns and chives and mix well. Allow to cool slightly, then spoon into barquettes. Garnish each portion with prawns and triangles of lemon.

Makes 12.

8 large hard-boiled eggs
100 g (3½ oz) can smoked peppered
mackerel, drained
6 teaspoons mayonnaise
2 teaspoons lemon juice
1 teaspoon chopped fresh parsley
1 teaspoon tomato purée (paste)
1 teaspoon Worcestershire sauce
salt and pepper
60 g (2 oz) peeled prawns, finely diced
shredded lettuce

TO GARNISH:

black and pink lumpfish roe
lemon triangles
dill sprigs

Shell eggs and halve lengthways. Take out yolks and divide equally between 2 bowls. Into one bowl, add smoked mackerel, 3 teaspoons mayonnaise, 1 teaspoon lemon juice and the parsley. Mash ingredients together and form a rough chunky paste.

In the second bowl, add remaining mayonnaise, and lemon juice, tomato purée (paste), Worcestershire sauce and mix well together. Season to taste with salt and pepper and stir in the chopped prawns. Fill half the eggs with the mackerel mixture and half with the prawn mixture. Arrange the eggs on a plate of shredded lettuce. Garnish the mackerel eggs with triangles of lemon and spoonfuls of black lumpfish roe and the prawn eggs with pink lumpfish roe and sprigs of dill.

Serves 4.

GLAZED CHICKEN WINGS

750 g (1½ lb) chicken wings
3 spring onions
3 tablespoons ginger wine
4 tablespoons dark soy sauce
2 teaspoons sugar
sesame seeds

Remove the tips from the chicken wings. These can be used to make stock for soup. The wings may be left or cut again at the joint into half.

Cut the spring onion into 5 cm (2 in) lengths and put into a large saucepan or a wok with the ginger wine and soy sauce. Add the sugar and bring to the boil. Place the chicken wings, in one layer, in this mixture.

Cover and simmer slowly for 20 minutes or until chicken is cooked through and tender when tested with a skewer. Turn the chicken over from time to time. Serve warm or cold. If liked, sprinkle with sesame seeds.

Makes 8-10.

CHICKEN TARRAGON SALAD

250 g (8 oz/4 cups) pasta shells
1.5 kg (3 lb) chicken, cooked
250 g (8 oz) seedless grapes
1 tablespoon chopped fresh tarragon
60 ml (2 fl oz/¼ cup) mayonnaise
60 ml (2 fl oz/¼ cup) crème fraîche
salt and pepper
sprigs of parsley, to garnish

In a large saucepan of boiling salted water, cook pasta shells until just tender. Drain, rinse in cold water, then drain again thoroughly.

Remove meat from chicken and cut into pieces. In a bowl, mix together pasta, chicken, grapes and tarragon.

In a bowl, mix together mayonnaise and crème fraîche. Season with salt and pepper. Pour over chicken and mix thoroughly. Serve salad at room temperature garnished with a few sprigs of parsley.

Serves 6.

TANDOORI CHICKEN

TANGY DRUMSTICKS

1.25 kg (2½ lb) chicken joints, skinned
3 teaspoons lime juice
salt
1 small onion
3 teaspoons Tandoori Masala, see below
2 teaspoons Garam Masala, see below
2.5 cm (1 in) piece root ginger, grated
315 ml (10 fl oz/1¼ cups) natural yogurt
lime wedges and coriander leaves, to garnish

Wash chicken joints and pat dry with absorbent kitchen paper, then slash meaty parts 2 or 3 times.

Place chicken in a shallow non-metal dish. Sprinkle with lime juice and salt and set aside. Put onion, masalas, ginger, salt and yogurt into a blender or food processor fitted with a metal blade and process until smooth and frothy. Pour over chicken and cover loosely. Leave to marinate in a cool place for 6 hours or overnight.

Preheat oven to 200C (400F/Gas 6). Drain excess marinade from chicken joints and place them in a roasting tin. Cook for 25-30 minutes, until tender and well browned. Serve hot, garnished with lime wedges and coriander.

Serves 4.

TANDOORI MASALA

3 teaspoons ground cumin seeds
3 teaspoons ground coriander seeds
3 teaspoons cayenne pepper
few drops red food colouring

Mix ingredients. Store in a small, airtight jar for up to 2 months.

GARAM MASALA

4 teaspoons cardamom seeds
two 7.5 cm (3 in) cinnamon sticks, crushed
2 teaspoons whole cloves
4 teaspoons black peppercorns
3 tablespoons cumin seeds
3 tablespoons coriander seeds

Fry spices over medium heat for 5-10 minutes, until browned, stirring. Cool, then grind to a fine powder. Store for up to 2 months.

1 small onion, chopped
1 tablespoon clear honey
1 clove garlic, crushed
3 tablespoons corn oil
3 tablespoons tomato ketchup (sauce)
1 tablespoon tomato purée (paste)
2 teaspoons Worcestershire sauce
1 teaspoon chilli sauce
2 pinches of Chinese five-spice powder
8 chicken drumsticks
cress and slices of lemon, to garnish

In a small saucepan, mix together onion, honey, garlic, 2 tablespoons oil, tomato ketchup (sauce) and purée (paste).

Add Worcestershire sauce, chilli sauce and five-spice powder and simmer, uncovered, for 5 minutes, stirring occasionally. Blend mixture to a smooth purée in a blender or food processor. Add remaining oil and stir well.

Arrange chicken drumsticks in a roasting tin. Brush with marinade and leave to marinate for 1 hour. Preheat oven to 200C (400F/Gas 6). Bake in oven for 35-40 minutes, turning and brushing frequently with marinade juices. Serve hot or cold, with cress and lemon slices.

Serves 4.

HAM & EGG LOAF

500 g (1 lb) cooked ham
90 g (3 oz) mushrooms
90 g (3 oz) dried stuffing mix
5 eggs
155 ml (5 fl oz/²⁄₃ cup) single (light) cream
2 teaspoons mushroom ketchup
1 tablespoon chopped fresh parsley
parsley sprigs, to garnish
crusty rolls, to serve

Preheat the oven to 190C (375F/Gas 5). Mince ham and mushrooms together and stir in the stuffing mix.

Put 3 eggs in a saucepan of cold water, bring to the boil and simmer for 10 minutes until hard. Plunge the eggs into cold water and then remove the shells.

Beat together remaining eggs, cream, mushrooms, ketchup and parsley, pour onto the ham mixture and stir well.

Put half the mixture into a 22.5 x 12.5 cm (9 x 5 in) loaf tin and arrange the hard-boiled eggs down the centre. Top with remaining ham and mushroom mixture and bake in the oven for 1 hour. Allow to cool completely, then turn out and slice thickly. Garnish with sprigs of parsley and serve with crusty rolls.

Serves 4.

SAUSAGE & APPLE PLAIT

315 g (10 oz) packet puff pastry, thawed if frozen
315 g (10 oz) sausagemeat
1 onion, very finely chopped
2 apples, very finely chopped
90 g (3 oz/³⁄₄ cup) apple and herb stuffing mix
1 egg, beaten
beaten egg, to glaze
1 tablespoon sesame seeds
thinly sliced apple and sage leaves, to garnish

Roll out pastry on a lightly floured surface to a 45 x 35 cm (18 x 14 in) rectangle and leave to rest. Meanwhile, preheat the oven to 200C (400F/Gas 6).

In a bowl, mix together sausagemeat, onion, apples, stuffing mix and egg. Pile sausage filling down centre of the pastry, leaving about 6 cm (2½ in) of pastry at the top and bottom and 10 cm (4 in) to each side of the filling. Brush the edges of the pastry with beaten egg and fold the top and bottom over the sausagemeat.

Make 7.5 cm (3 in) cuts at 1 cm (½ in) intervals down each side of the pastry, then fold one strip at a time over the filling from alternate sides until the sausagemeat is completely enclosed. Brush all over with beaten egg and sprinkle with the sesame seeds. Bake in the oven for 30 minutes until golden. Cut plait into thick slices and serve garnished with apple slices and sage leaves.

Serves 6-8.

STROGANOFF SALAD

375 g (12 oz) cold, rare cooked beef	
250 g (8 oz) button mushrooms, sliced	
6 spring onions, chopped or shredded	
1 red pepper (capsicum), seeded and sliced	
shredded lettuce, to serve	

SOUR CREAM DRESSING:

155 ml (5 fl oz/²⁄₃ cup) thick sour cream	
1 tablespoon horseradish sauce	
2 teaspoons lemon juice	
salt and pepper	

Cut the beef into thin strips and put into a bowl with the mushrooms, onions and pepper (capsicum).

To make the dressing, mix ingredients together in a bowl. Pour over the salad and toss gently. Line a serving dish with shredded lettuce and spoon salad on top.

Serves 4.

CHEF'S SALAD

½ iceberg lettuce	
½ Webb's lettuce	
4 sticks celery, sliced	
½ bunch radishes, sliced	
185 g (6 oz) cold cooked chicken	
125 g (4 oz) sliced ham	
125 g (4 oz) Emmental cheese	

BLUE CHEESE DRESSING:

3 tablespoons natural yogurt	
3 tablespoons mayonnaise	
60 g (2 oz) Danish blue or Roquefort cheese, rinded and crumbled	
1 teaspoon lemon juice	

Shred iceberg lettuce, tear the Webb's into smaller pieces and put into a salad bowl with the celery and radishes. Cut the chicken, ham and cheese into strips and add to the salad.

To make the dressing, put ingredients into a blender or food processor and work until smooth. Pour over salad and toss gently to coat all the leaves.

Serves 4.

GERMAN POTATO SALAD

1 kg (2 lb) potatoes, scrubbed
6 spring onions, finely chopped
salt and pepper
3 tablespoons mayonnaise
3 tablespoons natural yogurt
snipped chives, to garnish

Cook unpeeled potatoes in a saucepan of boiling salted water for about 15 minutes until tender.

Drain, then cool a little before removing skins. Cool completely.

Dice potatoes and put into a bowl with spring onions, then season with salt and pepper.

Mix mayonnaise and yogurt together in a bowl, then fold into the salad. Spoon into serving dish and serve garnished with chives.

Serves 6.

Note: The potato skins can be left on if preferred.

WINTER GREEN SALAD

1½ lettuces or mixed salad leaves
250 g (8 oz) broccoli flowerets, trimmed
1 bunch watercress, trimmed
440 g (14 oz) can artichoke hearts, drained
1 bulb fennel, finely sliced
1 green pepper (capsicum), seeded and sliced

GREEN GODDESS DRESSING:
155 ml (5 fl oz/⅔ cup) mayonnaise
2 anchovy fillets, drained and finely chopped
2 spring onions, finely chopped
2 tablespoons chopped fresh parsley
1 tablespoon tarragon vinegar
1 tablespoon lemon juice
1 clove garlic, crushed
3 tablespoons thick sour cream
salt and pepper

Tear the lettuces into small pieces and put into a serving bowl. Blanch broccoli in a saucepan of boiling water for 2 minutes. Drain, cool, then add to the lettuce with the watercress. Halve the artichoke hearts and add to the salad bowl with the sliced fennel and pepper (capsicum). Toss gently together.

To make the dressing, mix all the ingredients together in a bowl. Spoon a little dressing over the salad, and serve the remainder separately.

Serves 6-8.

Variation: Substitute cauliflower for the broccoli, if preferred.

SAFFRON RICE RING

CALIFORNIAN SALAD

30 g (1 oz/6 teaspoons) butter	
4 cardamom pods	
3 cloves	
5 cm (2 in) piece cinnamon stick	
250 g (8 oz/1¼ cups) basmati rice	
500 ml (16 fl oz/2 cups) hot chicken stock	
good pinch saffron threads	
125 g (4 oz) frozen petit pois	
salt and pepper	
3 tablespoons single (light) cream	
mint sprigs and peeled prawns,	
to garnish	

FILLING:

250 g (8 oz) peeled cooked prawns
½ cucumber, diced
60 ml (2 fl oz/¼ cup) natural yogurt
2 teaspoons chopped fresh mint
pinch cayenne pepper

In a large saucepan, melt butter, add cardamoms, cloves and cinnamon stick and fry for 1 minute. Stir in rice and cook for 1 minute. Gradually stir in hot chicken stock, keeping it simmering as it is added. Simmer rice for 15 minutes.

Meanwhile, put saffron into a cup, pour on 2 tablespoons hot water. Stir into rice with peas and continue to cook for 2 minutes. Remove from the heat and season to taste with salt and pepper.

Remove cardamoms, cloves and cinnamon stick, then stir in cream. Spoon rice into a 1.25 litre (2 pint/ 5 cup) ring mould, pressing down with the back of spoon. Cool, then refrigerate for 30 minutes.

Invert rice ring onto a plate. To make filling, mix all the ingredients together in a bowl, then spoon into centre of rice ring. Serve garnished with sprigs of mint and prawns.

Serves 4-6.

6 teaspoons powdered gelatine
4 teaspoons sugar
2 lemons
3 tablespoons wine vinegar
few drops yellow food colouring
250 g (8 oz) fresh asparagus, cooked
1 large avocado
2 large carrots, grated
fresh herbs, to garnish

Sprinkle gelatine over 90 ml (3 fl oz/ ⅓ cup) water in a small bowl and leave to soften for 2-3 minutes. Stand bowl in a saucepan of hot water and stir until dissolved. Stir in sugar, then set aside to cool.

Grate the peel from one of the lemons and squeeze the juice from both. Reserve 1 tablespoon lemon juice. Put the grated peel and remaining juice into a measuring jug and make up to 940 ml (30 fl oz/ 3¾ cups) with water. Add dissolved gelatine, the vinegar and a few drops of yellow food colouring. Pour a little of the liquid into a 1.8 litre (3 pint/7½ cup) ring mould and refrigerate until the jelly has set.

Cut the tips off the asparagus and arrange on the set jelly. Halve avocado, remove stone, peel, then dice flesh. Place in a bowl and mix with reserved lemon juice. Chop asparagus stalks and add to the avocado with the carrots. Mix well. Stir in remaining liquid, then spoon into the mould. Refrigerate until set.

To serve, turn out the vegetable ring onto a plate and garnish with herbs.

Serves 8.

QUICK DIPS

MEXICAN BEAN DIP

CREAMY CORN DIP

300 g (10 oz) jar corn relish
300 ml (10 fl oz) carton thick sour cream
biscuits (crackers, or corn chips, to serve

Mix the jar of corn relish with the sour cream. Pile into a serving bowl and surround with biscuits or corn chips.

Serves 6-8.

CAVIAR DIP

300 ml (10 fl oz) carton thick sour cream
50 g (1½ oz) jar red caviar
1 tablespoon finely chopped onion
fresh parsley sprig, to garnish
vegetables and biscuits (crackers), to serve

Mix the sour cream with half the caviar and the onion. Turn into a serving bowl and swirl in the rest of the caviar. Garnish with a parsley sprig and serve with vegetables or biscuits for dipping.

Serves 6-8.

ANCHOVY DIP

300 ml (10 fl oz) carton thick sour cream
45 g (1½ oz) can anchovy fillets, drained and mashed
3 tablespoons chopped dill pickles
2 teaspoons drained capers
biscuits (crackers), to serve

Blend sour cream, anchovies and pickles. Turn into a bowl and garnish with the capers. Serve with biscuits.

Serves 6-8.

465 g (15 oz) canned red kidney beans
2 tablespoons vegetable oil
90 g (3 oz/¾ cup) grated Cheddar cheese
½ teaspoon salt
1 teaspoon chilli powder
1 tablespoon chopped green pepper (capsicum)
corn chips or prawn crisps for dipping

Drain the beans, reserving the liquid for the dip.

Heat the oil in a small pan and add the beans, mashing with a potato masher as they cook. Add 3 tablespoons of the reserved bean liquid and stir in until well mixed. Cool. Add cheese, salt and chilli powder. If the mixture is thick, add more of the reserved bean liquid until it is a good consistency for scooping. Add the pepper. Serve hot with corn chips or prawn crisps.

Serves 4-6.

FRIED PRAWN CRISPS

If using prawn crisps, drop a few at a time into deep hot oil. When they come to the top, remove almost immediately and drain. The crisps take only a few seconds to cook. Drain on absorbent paper and store in an airtight container until ready to use.

BAGNA CAUDA

MINTED SAMBAL DIP

2 or 3 carrots
½ cauliflower
other raw vegetables in season
45 g (1½ oz) canned anchovy fillets
125 g (4 oz) butter
125 ml (4 fl oz/½ cup) virgin olive oil or vegetable oil
4 cloves garlic, crushed
250 ml (8 fl oz/1 cup) double (thick) cream
slices of crusty bread, to serve

Prepare the vegetables first: peel carrots and cut into 10 cm (4 in) length sticks; separate the cauliflower into florets and prepare other vegetables.

Drain the anchovies, chop and mash well. Melt the butter with the oil in a small pan and add the anchovies and garlic. Bring the mixture to a gentle boil, stirring all the time, and simmer for 5 minutes. Add the cream to the anchovy mixture. Heat gently, stirring while it thickens, for about 5 minutes.

Serve the anchovy sauce in a bowl while still hot. Provide wooden toothpicks for guests to spear their chosen vegetables, dip into the hot sauce and eat with a slice of crusty bread.

Serves 4-6.

4 spring onions
300 ml (10 fl oz) carton thick sour cream
1 teaspoon finely grated fresh root ginger
1 tablespoon lemon juice
1 tablespoon curry powder
6-8 tablespoons chopped fresh mint
1 clove garlic
1 teaspoon salt
fresh vegetables for dipping

Finely chop the spring onions including most of the green tops. Add to the sour cream with the ginger, lemon juice, curry powder and chopped mint. Mix well.

Peel garlic and crush the clove in salt until it forms a pulp. Add to the sour cream mixture and stir in well. If mixture is thin, whip until thickened. The flavour will improve if dip is chilled for at least 24 hours.

Select crisp fresh vegetables for the crudités. Peel and cut into 10 cm (4 in) lengths. Serve chilled with the dip. Suitable crudités are carrots and celery sticks, mange tout (snow peas), radishes, spring onions, blanched broccoli and cauliflower florets.

Serves 6-8.

CHARLOTTE RUSSE

16 sponge fingers
3 teaspoons powdered gelatine
4 egg yolks
90 g (3 oz/⅓ cup) caster sugar
625 ml (20 fl oz/2½ cups) whipping cream
1 vanilla pod, split open
315 ml (10 fl oz/1¼ cups) thick sour cream
185 g (6 oz) fresh raspberries
whipped cream, to decorate

Line the base of 1.1 litre (35 fl oz/ 4¼ cup) charlotte mould with greaseproof paper. Stand sponge fingers, pressing against each other, round sides of mould and trim to fit.

Sprinkle gelatine over 3 tablespoons of water in a small bowl and leave to soften for 2-3 minutes. In a bowl, whisk egg yolks and sugar together until thick and mousselike. Put 375 ml (12 fl oz/1½ cups) whipping cream in a saucepan with vanilla pod and bring almost to boiling point. Strain over egg mixture, stirring well. Pour back into saucepan and stir over low heat until mixture has thickened slightly. Do not boil.

Strain into clean bowl and add soaked gelatine. Stir until dissolved. Cool, then stand bowl in larger bowl of iced water and stir until mixture thickens. Whip remaining cream with sour cream and fold into mixture. Pour into prepared mould, cover with plastic wrap and refrigerate overnight. When ready to serve, turn out onto serving plate, remove greaseproof paper and decorate with the raspberries and whipped cream. Tie a ribbon round pudding.

Serves 6-8.

TART LEMON MOULD

625 ml (20 fl oz/2½ cups) milk
90 g (3 oz/⅓ cup) granulated sugar
3 teaspoons powdered gelatine
3 small egg yolks
grated peel and juice of 1 large lemon
90 g (3 oz/⅓ cup) caster sugar
lemon twists and herb sprigs, to decorate

Put milk, granulated sugar and gelatine into a small saucepan and set over a low heat. Bring almost to boiling point (but do not boil), stirring constantly. Remove from heat.

In a bowl, beat egg yolks together lightly and gradually pour hot milk over them, stirring all the time. Pour into a 940 ml (30 fl oz/3¾ cup) mould. Leave mixture at room temperature until cold, then refrigerate until set.

While mixture is cooling, put grated lemon peel and juice into a small saucepan with caster sugar and stir over a low heat until sugar has dissolved. Leave to cool. When ready to serve, turn out pudding onto a serving plate and pour lemon syrup around it. Decorate with lemon twists and herbs.

Serves 4.

COFFEE BOMBE

3 eggs, separated
185 g (6 oz/¾ cup) caster sugar
75 ml (2½ fl oz/⅓ cup) cold strong black coffee
500 ml (16 fl oz/2 cups) double (thick) cream
155 g (5 oz) meringues
whipped cream and chocolate coffee beans, to decorate
hot Bitter Mocha Sauce, see below

In a large bowl, beat egg yolks and sugar together until thick and mousse-like. Gently stir in coffee. In a separate bowl, whip cream lightly. Crush meringues.

Fold cream and meringues into coffee mixture. In a large bowl, whisk egg whites until stiff and fold 1 tablespoon into coffee mixture. Tip egg whites onto coffee mixture, then fold carefully. Pour into a 2 litre (64 fl oz/8 cup) lightly oiled bombe mould and freeze until firm.

One hour before serving, transfer the bombe to the refrigerator to soften slightly. Turn out onto a serving dish and decorate with cream and chocolate coffee beans. Serve with hot Bitter Mocha Sauce handed separately.

Serves 8.

Note: To turn out bombe, wring out a tea-towel in very hot water, wrap around mould and invert.

BITTER MOCHA SAUCE

90 g (3 oz) bitter plain (dark) chocolate
1 tablespoon dark, very strong, coarsely ground expresso coffee grounds
315 ml (10 fl oz/1¼ cups) whipping cream
7 g (¼ oz/1½ teaspoons) butter

Break chocolate into small pieces and place in the top of a double boiler or a bowl. Set aside. Put coffee and cream into a saucepan, bring to boil, then remove and leave to infuse for 30 minutes.

Strain creamy coffee through a fine sieve onto the chocolate. Place over a pan of simmering water and stir until chocolate has melted. Whisk in butter and serve.

FRUIT CASKET

WHISKED SPONGE:
6 eggs
185 g (6 oz/¾ cup) caster sugar
finely grated peel of 1 lemon or small orange
185 g (6 oz/1½ cups) self-raising flour
icing sugar, to serve

FILLING:
315 ml (10 fl oz/1¼ cups) whipping cream
1 tablespoon kirsch
caster sugar, to taste
250 g (8 oz) raspberries
450 g (1 lb) strawberries

Preheat oven to 180C (350F/Gas 4). Grease a 22.5 cm (9 in) cake tin and dust with sugar, then flour.

In a large bowl, whisk the eggs, sugar and lemon or orange peel until very thick, pale and mousse-like. Setting the bowl over a saucepan of gently simmering water helps with whisking, but continue to whisk until the mix is cold.

Sift flour twice onto a plate, then carefully, but thoroughly, fold into egg mixture. Pour into the prepared tin. Bake in the oven for 15-20 minutes, until lightly golden and springy. Cool on a wire rack.

To prepare filling, in a large bowl, whip cream until stiff and fold in kirsch and sugar. Fold in half of raspberries. Slice strawberries and set aside.

Cut cool sponge cake horizontally through centre. Put bottom half on a serving dish. Cut a square out of remaining half to leave a 2.5 cm (1 inch) unbroken frame.

Place frame exactly on top of cake half. Fill frame with whipped cream mixture and top with sliced strawberries and remaining raspberries. Cut remaining piece of sponge cake diagonally in half and set on top like butterfly wings. Dust with icing sugar. Serve within 1 hour. Garnish with red currants, if desired.

Serves 8.

Variation: Decorate cake with whipped cream, toasted sliced almonds and strawberry slices.

BARBECUES

The great advantage to holding a barbecue party is that, by its very nature, the occasion is relaxed and informal. There is also something mouth-watering about food cooked over hot coals. Even the most ordinary dish can taste simply delicious when eaten 'al fresco' on a sunny afternoon or warm evening.

Lunch-time barbecues can be great family events. Children have more freedom to run around and adults can relax in the garden. You can also arrange games such as croquet or volleyball or even a swimming party if you have a pool. Evening barbecues are probably best reserved for more adult occasions. Burn insect repellent sticks and string up coloured lights around the patio or garden to create a festive atmosphere.

Although the host should take responsibility for cooking the food, a barbecue is an excellent opportunity to share the load. Most friends usually enjoy taking turns with the barbecue, which will allow you to attend to other guests or simply enjoy the party.

PREPARING THE FOOD

As with any party, a vital ingredient of its success is careful planning. Virtually all the side dishes, salads and desserts can be prepared in advance, leaving you free to tend to the barbecue itself. All marinated meat and fish dishes or skewered meat should be in the refrigerator and ready for cooking.

Place the side dishes, plates and cutlery on a large table either in the shelter of the terrace or just inside the door leading to the garden. Paper or plastic plates and paper napkins are ideal, but try to avoid plastic cutlery as it tends to break easily. Finally, provide plenty of large waste disposal sacks at obvious and convenient locations.

PREPARING THE BARBECUE

There are many kinds of barbecue grills, and, depending on which you use, you do not even have to go outside to cook barbecued food. Some electric grills are suitable for indoor cooking. Charcoal or gas grills with hoods can be used outside even in inclement weather.

If you are using a charcoal-burning barbecue, make sure you begin preparation well before you plan to eat. Position the barbecue in a secure and convenient place (a heated barbecue is very difficult to move). The coals will probably take 30-40 minutes to become hot enough; when the

Above: There are three basic varieties of barbecues: the kettle barbecue which uses charcoal and needs starter fuel, and gas and electric barbecues, which both use lava bricks. Other useful accessories are smokers, wire baskets, and long-handled tongs, brushes, skewers and spatulas.

flames have died down and the charcoal is covered with a white ash, it is time to commence cooking. You may want to use lava bricks as they take only a few minutes to heat up sufficiently. Charcoal will burn for about 1½ hours. Additional pieces of charcoal can be placed around the edges to maintain the heat.

Heat can be adjusted to high, medium or low depending on the food being cooked. To test the heat of your barbecue, carefully place an open hand over the coals. If you can keep your hand a few inches above the coals for as long as five seconds, the temperature is low; three to four seconds is medium, and two seconds is hot. On a hooded barbecue, heat is greater when the lid is lowered. If you need less heat, push the food away from the centre of the grill, or push the coals aside to distribute their heat. To make the fire hotter, push the coals together and gently fan the coals.

Although each recipe in this chapter has a cooking time, it should be regarded as a guide only. There are so many variables to consider, such as the thickness of the meat and the type and heat of the coals. One of the great pleasures of barbecuing is that it is not a precise science, but a chance to let the cook's individuality shine through.

Fish-shaped wire baskets enable whole fish to be turned over half way through cooking without damaging them.

Rectangular or square hinged wire baskets are perfect for barbecuing cuts of meats or sliced vegetables.

For barbecuing chunks of meat, fish, vegetables or fruit, use long skewers with either square edges or ridges.

CHIVE & GARLIC BREAD

| 1 French loaf |
| 3 cloves garlic |
| ¼ teaspoon salt |
| 125 g (4 oz/½ cup) butter |
| 2 tablespoons chopped fresh chives |

Slice loaf diagonally and deeply at about 2 cm (¾ in) intervals, but do not cut through completely.

Peel garlic, place on a piece of greaseproof paper, sprinkle with salt and crush with flat side of a table knife. Soften butter, blend in garlic and mix in chives. Spread garlic butter between slices, covering both sides generously.

Re-shape loaf and wrap securely in foil. Place on rack and barbecue over hot coals for 10-15 minutes, turning parcel over several times. Open foil and serve at once.

Serves 6.

PIADINA

| 345 g (11 oz/2½ cups) strong white plain flour |
| 1 heaped teaspoon salt |
| ½ teaspoon baking powder |
| 75 ml (2½ fl oz/⅓ cup) milk |
| 3 tablespoons olive oil |

TO SERVE:

| salami, cheese and salad |

In a bowl, mix flour with salt and baking powder. Mix milk with 75 ml (2½ fl oz/⅓ cup) water. Add oil and a little of the water and milk mixture to flour mixture. Stir with a fork and gradually add more liquid until it has all been incorporated. Mix to form a soft dough.

Turn onto a lightly floured surface and knead until smooth. Allow to rest for 15 minutes. Divide dough into 12 equal pieces. Roll each piece out to a circle measuring 7.5 cm (3 in) in diameter.

Heat a heavy-based frying pan or griddle until a drop of water flicked on the surface bounces and evaporates. Place 2-3 circles in pan or on griddle and cook for 30 seconds. Flip over and continue cooking.

Turn each circle 2 or 3 times until sides are speckled with brown. Place on wire rack while cooking remainder. Serve warm with salami, cheese and salad.

Serves 4-6.

RICH TOMATO BASTE

1 large red pepper (capsicum), seeded and finely chopped

500 g (1 lb) tomatoes, skinned and chopped

1 small onion, finely chopped

1 clove garlic, finely chopped

155 ml (5 fl oz/²⁄₃ cup) dry white wine

large rosemary sprig

2 tablespoons sunflower oil

salt and pepper

Put first six ingredients in a saucepan. Simmer, uncovered, until thickened; purée. Add oil and seasoning.

SWEET & SOUR MARINADE

grated peel and juice of 1 orange

155 ml (5 fl oz/²⁄₃ cup) clear honey

155 ml (5 fl oz/²⁄₃ cup) red wine vinegar

3 tablespoons soy sauce

3 tablespoons Worcestershire sauce

1 tablespoon sesame oil

Combine all ingredients in a saucepan. Bring to the boil, then simmer, uncovered, for 5 minutes until sauce reduces by about one-third.

COGNAC MARINADE

4 tablespoons brandy

155 ml (5 fl oz/²⁄₃ cup) dry white wine

2 tablespoons olive oil

60 g (2 oz) tiny button mushrooms, finely sliced

2 shallots, finely chopped

1 teaspoon fresh thyme leaves

4 bay leaves

1 small clove garlic, crushed

10 peppercorns, crushed

1 teaspoon salt

Combine ingredients in a lidded container. Leave for 24 hours. Strain.

WARMLY-SPICED BASTE

75 g (2½ oz/¼ cup, plus 3 teaspoons) dark soft brown sugar

2 tablespoons red wine vinegar

¼ teaspoon ground cloves

¼ teaspoon dry mustard

1½ teaspoons ground allspice

3 teaspoons cornflour

1 small eating apple, peeled, cored and finely chopped

Place ingredients in a saucepan. Add 220 ml (7 fl oz/⅞ cup) water. Bring to the boil, stirring; simmer for 5 minutes or until thickened.

FIERY CHILLI BASTE

30 g (1 oz/2 tablespoons) muscovado sugar

155 ml (5 fl oz/²⁄₃ cup) tomato ketchup (sauce)

185 ml (6 fl oz/¾ cup) cider vinegar

2 tablespoons Worcestershire sauce

2 teaspoons chilli powder

¼ onion, finely chopped

Put sugar and 155 ml (5 fl oz/²⁄₃ cup) water in heavy-based saucepan. Stir until dissolved. Add remaining ingredients; bring to boil. Simmer until reduced by about one-third.

CITRUS SHARP MARINADE

grated peel and juice of 4 limes

grated peel and juice of 1 lemon

2 teaspoons salt

6 tablespoons sunflower oil

12 white peppercorns, bruised

Mix all ingredients together in a bowl, cover and leave to infuse for 8 hours, or overnight. Strain marinade before using.

Note: All the recipes given here make 315 ml (10 fl oz/1¼ cups).

POTTERS RED RELISH

4 large ripe tomatoes
1 small red pepper (capsicum), seeded
1 small green pepper (capsicum), seeded
1 large onion
2 teaspoons salt
90 g (3 oz/½ cup) dark soft brown sugar
155 ml (5 fl oz/⅔ cup) malt vinegar
½ teaspoon sweet paprika
parsley, to garnish

Peel tomatoes and finely chop. Very finely chop red and green peppers (capsicums) and onion.

Put all the ingredients, except the garnish, into a heavy-based saucepan. Bring to boil, then reduce heat and simmer gently, stirring frequently for 1 hour or until mixture is thick.

Pour into a large jam jar, cover with a waxed disc and jam pot cover and leave for 1-2 weeks before using. Serve in a bowl, garnished with parsley.

Makes about 500 g (1 lb).

Note: This spicy relish is delicious served with meat and game.

BARBECUE SAUCE

3 tablespoons corn oil
1 small onion
1 clove garlic, crushed
½ teaspoon dry mustard
2 tablespoons malt vinegar
1 tablespoon Worcestershire sauce
2 tablespoons light soft brown sugar
3 tablespoons tomato ketchup (sauce)
½ teaspoon chilli seasoning
185 ml (6 fl oz/¾ cup) chicken stock
sprig of parsley, to garnish

Heat oil in a small saucepan. Add onion and garlic and cook gently for 2 minutes, stirring frequently.

Stir in mustard, vinegar, Worcestershire sauce, sugar, tomato ketchup (sauce), chilli and chicken stock. Bring to the boil.

Cover and simmer sauce gently for 7-8 minutes until slightly thickened. Serve hot as a sauce, garnished with sprigs of parsley, with beefburgers, hot dogs or fried chicken. Or, if preferred, allow to cool and use to brush over meats, poultry and fish while baking or grilling.

Makes 315 ml (10 fl oz/1¼ cups).

RED MULLET WITH FENNEL

TARAMA SARDINES

| four 250 g (8 oz) red mullet |
| fennel leaves, to garnish |

| MARINADE: |
| 4 tablespoons salad oil |
| 1 teaspoon lemon juice |
| 1 teaspoon fennel seeds |
| ¼ teaspoon sea salt |
| ¼ teaspoon pepper |

Mix marinade ingredients together in a large shallow dish.

Scrape away hard scales, remove gills and fins and clean inside of fish, but do not remove liver. Rinse, drain and wipe dry with absorbent kitchen paper. Score through the skin twice on each side. Put fish in marinade and leave for 1 hour, basting occasionally.

Drain fish and lay on a wire rack over hot coals and barbecue for 6-8 minutes on each side, basting occasionally with marinade to prevent sticking and encourage browning. Garnish with fennel leaves.

Serves 4.

Note: To speed up cooking an oiled tray may be inverted over fish.

| 6 fresh sardines |
| 2 tablespoons lemon juice |
| pepper |
| 3-4 tablespoons taramasalata |
| parsley sprigs, to garnish |

Cut off and discard sardine heads and, using a small skewer or teaspoon, carefully clean out inside of each fish. Rinse and pat dry on absorbent kitchen paper.

Brush inside sardines with lemon juice and season to taste with black pepper. Carefully fill cavities with the taramasalata.

Place sardines in a hinged rectangular basket and barbecue over hot coals for 3-4 minutes on each side. Arrange sardines in a spoke design on a round wooden platter. Garnish by inserting sprigs of parsley into the taramasalata.

Serves 6.

Variation: Use small trout if sardines are not available and double the quantity of taramasalata.

MEDITERRANEAN KING PRAWNS

AROMATIC GRILLED SALMON

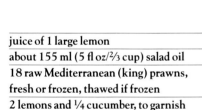

juice of 1 large lemon
about 155 ml (5 fl oz/²⁄₃ cup) salad oil
18 raw Mediterranean (king) prawns, fresh or frozen, thawed if frozen
2 lemons and ¼ cucumber, to garnish

To prepare the garnish remove tops and bottoms from lemons and slice middle sections thinly. Using a canelle knife, remove equidistant strips of cucumber skin lengthwise. Thinly slice cucumber. Curve cucumber slices round lemon slices before threading onto wooden cocktail sticks.

Put lemon juice in one shallow dish and oil in another. Dip prawns, 2 or 3 at a time, into lemon juice. Shake off surplus juice, then dip into the oil.

Barbecue prawns on a rack over hot coals for 10-12 minutes, brushing frequently with remaining oil. Serve hot, garnished with lemon and cucumber sticks, and have finger-bowls nearby.

Serves 6.

Note: Buy whole, unpeeled king prawns for grilling. The grey-brown translucent appearance of these prawns changes to orangey-pink when cooked.

six 185 g (6 oz) middle cut salmon cutlets, 2 cm (¾ in) thick
salt and pepper
flour
125 g (4 oz/½ cup) butter
a handful of winter savory or 1-2 tablespoons dried winter savory, moistened
6 teaspoons lumpfish caviar
winter savory or tarragon, to garnish

Rinse salmon and pat dry on absorbent kitchen paper. Season to taste with salt and pepper; dip in flour and shake off surplus.

Melt butter and brush over salmon steaks. Place in a rectangular hinged basket. Sprinkle the winter savory over the coals when they are hot.

Barbecue fish on rack over hot coals for 4-5 minutes on each side, basting occasionally with melted butter. If the cutlets start to brown too quickly, reduce heat or move basket to side of barbecue. The cutlets are cooked when it is easy to move centre bone. Serve sprinkled with lumpfish caviar and garnish with winter savory or tarragon.

Serves 6.

PLOUGHMAN'S BURGERS

FILLET STEAK ENVELOPES

3 eggs
½ teaspoon pepper
1.5 kg (3 lb) freshly minced lean beef
4-6 tablespoons bottled fruity sauce
250 g (8 oz) Emmental cheese
shredded iceberg lettuce, to garnish

Beat the eggs in a large bowl, season to taste with pepper and mix in the minced beef.

Form the mixture into 24 thin burgers. Spread 12 of the burgers with sauce, leaving a border. Slice the cheese thinly and cut out 12 circles smaller than the burgers. Lay slices of cheese over the sauce, topping with the cheese trimmings. Cover with the remaining burgers and press the edges together to seal. Cook on rack over hot coals for 8-10 minutes on each side. Garnish with shredded lettuce and serve with Potters Red Relish (see page 31).

Makes 12.

four 185 g (6 oz) fillet steaks
185 g (6 oz) veal escalope
125 g (4 oz/½ cup) butter, softened
4 cloves garlic, crushed
1 teaspoon dried basil
salt and pepper

Using a rolling pin or milk bottle, flatten steaks between sheets of waxed or non-stick paper to 1 cm (½ in) thickness. Beat the veal thinly and cut into 4 equal pieces.

Make a deep horizontal slit through each steak to form a pocket. Mix the butter, garlic and basil thoroughly together and season to taste with salt and pepper. Spread half the butter mixture inside each pocket, then insert a piece of veal into each.

Spread the outside of steaks with remaining butter mixture. Cook on grill rack over hot coals for 2 minutes on each side to seal. Position steaks away from fierce heat and cook over medium coals for a further 6-8 minutes on each side, depending on taste.

Serves 4.

BROCHETTES MEXICANA

HOT DOGS WITH MUSTARD DIP

375 g (12 oz) trimmed rump steak	
375 g (12 oz) pork fillet	
1 large red pepper (capsicum), seeded	
1 large green pepper (capsicum), seeded	

MARINADE:

2 fresh green chillies, seeded	
250 g (8 oz) can tomatoes	
250 g (8 oz) can pimentos, drained	
2 tablespoons lemon juice	
2 tablespoons olive oil	
1 clove garlic, crushed	
1 teaspoon turmeric	
½-1 teaspoon salt	
½ teaspoon pepper	

Cut meat into 2.5 cm (1in) cubes. Then cut peppers (capsicums) into similar-sized pieces.

Purée the marinade ingredients, then simmer in a saucepan until reduced by half. Leave until cold. Stir in meat and peppers (capsicums). Cover and marinate in a cool place for 12 hours.

Thread meat onto skewers, alternating with red and green pepper (capsicum) pieces. Barbecue on rack over hot coals for about 20 minutes, turning frequently and basting with the marinade. Serve with corn or taco chips.

Serves 5-6.

12-16 frankfurters	
salt and pepper	

DIP:

3 tablespoons dry mustard	
250 ml (8 fl oz/1 cup) single (light) cream	

To make the dip, blend the dry mustard and cream together in a bowl. Cover and leave in a cool place for 15 minutes, for the flavour to mature.

Prick the frankfurters and grill on an oiled rack over medium coals for 6-10 minutes, turning frequently. Season to taste with salt and pepper.

Wrap a twist of coloured foil round one end of each frankfurter to make it easier to hold and arrange on a platter with a bowl of dip in the centre. If preferred, cooked frankfurters can be coated with dip and inserted into long soft rolls.

Makes 12-16.

DEEP SOUTH DRUMSTICKS

CHICKEN TERIYAKI

12-16 chicken drumsticks
2.5 cm (1 in) slice wholemeal bread
6 tablespoons tomato purée (paste)
3 tablespoons full-bodied red wine
juice of ½ lemon
2 tablespoons Worcestershire sauce
2 tablespoons molasses
1 teaspoon salt
½ teaspoon pepper
1 teaspoon French mustard
½ teaspoon chilli powder
1 teaspoon paprika
2 tablespoons oil
parsley sprigs, to garnish

Wash and dry drumsticks and set aside.

Remove the crusts, then dice the bread. Put in a large shallow dish, with all the remaining ingredients, except parsley. Stir with a fork until the bread is incorporated. (The mixture will be thick.) Put the drumsticks into the sauce, twisting at the bone end to coat evenly. Leave in a cool place for 1 hour, turning drumsticks occasionally.

Wrap drumsticks individually in oiled, single thickness foil. Barbecue on a rack over medium hot coals for 30-40 minutes, turning the packets from time to time. Test that a drumstick is done by pricking with a skewer – the juices should run clear and flesh touching the bone be fully cooked. Garnish with parsley and serve in the foil pockets with baby corn.

Serves 12-16.

750 g (1½ lb) boned, skinned chicken breasts
three 250 g (8 oz) cans water chestnuts
4 tablespoons dry sherry
4 tablespoons medium-dry white wine
4 tablespoons shoyu sauce
2 cloves garlic, crushed
sunflower oil for brushing
shredded lettuce, onion rings, parsley sprigs and paprika, to garnish, if desired

Cut the chicken into 2.5 cm (1 in) cubes. Drain water chestnuts and mix together in a dish.

In a small bowl, mix together sherry, wine, shoyu sauce and garlic. Pour over chicken and water chestnuts, cover and leave to marinate for 30-60 minutes, stirring occasionally. Using a slotted spoon, remove chicken cubes and water chestnuts from marinade. Thread pieces of chicken and water chestnuts alternately onto 8 long skewers. Reserve any remaining marinade.

Brush chicken and chestnuts with oil and barbecue on a rack over hot coals for about 10 minutes, turning frequently and basting with reserved marinade and oil. Arrange shredded lettuce on a large platter and place skewers in a criss-cross pattern on top. Garnish with raw onion rings, parsley and a sprinkling of paprika, if desired.

Serves 8.

LAMB CHOPS TAMARIND

45 g (1½ oz/3 tablespoons) butter
1 onion, finely chopped
2 tablespoons tamarind concentrate
2 tablespoons tomato purée (paste)
2.5 cm (1 in) piece fresh ginger root, finely grated
2 teaspoons dark soft brown sugar
2 tablespoons olive oil
grated peel and juice of 1 large orange
6 double loin lamb chops
orange segments, orange peel and parsley sprigs, to garnish

Melt the butter in a saucepan and cook onion until transparent.

Add tamarind concentrate, tomato purée (paste), ginger root, sugar, oil and orange peel and juice and simmer gently, uncovered, for 7-8 minutes until reduced by a quarter. Leave to cool. Coat the chops thoroughly in the sauce, then cover and refrigerate overnight.

Grill the chops on a rack over hot coals for 15-20 minutes, turning twice during cooking and basting frequently with remaining sauce. If there is insufficient sauce for basting use a little olive oil instead. Serve garnished with orange segments and peel and parsley.

Serves 6.

ORIENTAL SPARE RIBS

3 kg (6 lb) lean pork spare ribs
spring onion tassels, to garnish

SAUCE:
125 ml (4 fl oz/½ cup) hoisin sauce
125 ml (4 fl oz/½ cup) miso paste
315 ml (10 fl oz/1¼ cups) tomato purée (paste)
1½ teaspoons ground ginger
1½ teaspoons Chinese five-spice powder
185 g (6 oz/1 cup) muscovado sugar
3 cloves garlic, crushed
1 teaspoon salt
2 tablespoons saki (rice wine) or dry sherry

Separate the ribs and trim away most of the fat.

In a bowl, combine sauce ingredients and spread all over the ribs. Put the sauced ribs in a large shallow dish. Cover and leave in the refrigerator for at least 4 hours, or preferably overnight.

Place a drip pan in medium hot coals and barbecue ribs on a rack above the pan for 45-60 minutes, turning occasionally and basting with sauce. Heat any remaining sauce gently and serve separately. Garnish with onion tassels.

Serves 8.

Note: Offer guests warmed damp cloths or sachets of finger wipes.

VEGETABLE BAR

SUMMER RATATOUILLE

250 g (8 oz) even-shaped carrots
1 cauliflower
250 g (8 oz) mange tout (snow peas)
250 g (8 oz) baby onions
3 corn cobs (narrow in diameter)
1 tablespoon milk
salad oil

Prepare the vegetables. Using a small paring knife, cut carrots into chunks and shape into barrels. Separate cauliflower into flowerets.

Top and tail mange tout (snow peas), removing any tough strings. Peel onions. Using a heavy, sharp knife, cut sweetcorn into 2.5 cm (1 in) slices. Separately plunge vegetables into boiling water to which 1 tablespoon milk has been added. Cook to slightly soften or until al dente. Drain in a colander under cold running water, then drain again. Arrange in separate salad bowls.

Have ready 8-10 skewers and oil for brushing. After threading a selection of vegetables onto skewers, baste with oil and barbecue on a rack over hot coals for 5 minutes, turning skewers frequently. Serve with bowls of sauces and allow guests to help themselves.

Serves 8-10.

Note: The vegetables can also be served with dips such as garlic-flavoured mayonnaise.

60 ml (2 fl oz/¼ cup) virgin olive oil
1 bulb fennel, sliced
1 large onion, sliced
1 clove garlic, crushed
1 large beefsteak tomato, peeled and chopped
1 red pepper (capsicum), seeded
1 yellow pepper (capsicum), seeded
1 green pepper (capsicum), seeded
375 g (12 oz) courgettes (zucchini), sliced
1 teaspoon chopped fresh thyme
salt and pepper
shredded basil leaves and fennel fronds, to garnish

Heat oil in a large saucepan, add fennel, onion and garlic, cover and cook gently for 5 minutes. Add tomato; cook for 10 minutes.

Cut peppers (capsicums) into squares, add to pan with courgettes (zucchini) and thyme. Season with salt and pepper and cook for a further 5 minutes. Leave to cool.

Spoon the salad into a serving dish and serve garnished with basil leaves and fennel fronds.

Serves 6.

MALAYSIAN SALAD

AVOCADO & CITRUS SALAD

250 g (8 oz) white cabbage, shredded	
125 g (4 oz) thin green beans, cut into 2.5 cm (1 in) lengths	
½ small cauliflower, divided into flowerets	
125 g (4 oz) beansprouts, trimmed	
½ cucumber	
coriander leaves, to garnish	

PEANUT SAUCE:

30 g (1 oz) desiccated coconut
155 ml (5 fl oz/⅔ cup) boiling water
3 tablespoons peanut butter
2 teaspoons soy sauce
juice of ½ lime
¼ teaspoon chilli powder

To make sauce, place coconut in a bowl, pour over boiling water and leave to soak for 15 minutes.

Bring a large saucepan of water to the boil, add cabbage, beans and cauliflower and simmer for 2-3 minutes. Drain vegetables thoroughly, arrange on a platter or 4 individual plates. Scatter over beansprouts. Cut strips of skin from cucumber with a canelle knife, then slice the cucumber and arrange over salad.

Strain coconut milk into a bowl, discard the coconut, and add remaining sauce ingredients; mix well. Spoon onto centre of salad or serve separately. Garnish the salad with coriander leaves.

Serves 4.

½ curly endive, torn into pieces
2 oranges
1 grapefruit
1 ripe avocado

CITRUS DRESSING:

3 teaspoons sunflower oil
peel and juice of ½ lime
1 tablespoon chopped fresh mint
salt and pepper

Put endive into a salad bowl. Cut peel and pith from oranges and grapefruit. Holding each one over a bowl to catch juice, remove segments and halve. Arrange on top of endive.

Halve avocado, remove stone, slice or dice flesh, then add to salad.

To make the dressing, mix all the ingredients in a bowl or screw-top jar with 2 tablespoons of juice. Spoon over salad, and serve.

Serves 4.

FRENCH POTATO SALAD

SAGE & CREAM JACKETS

750 g (1½ lb) new potatoes, scrubbed
1 tablespoon virgin olive oil
2 tablespoons chopped mixed herbs and herb sprigs

HERB VINAIGRETTE:
3 tablespoons virgin olive oil
1 tablespoon white wine vinegar
salt and pepper

Boil unpeeled potatoes in a sauce-pan of salted water for about 15 minutes until tender. Drain. If they are small leave whole, otherwise cool a little, then cut into slices, halves or quarters. Put into a bowl and, while still warm, pour over 1 tablespoon oil. Leave to cool.

To make the dressing, mix together oil and vinegar in a bowl or screw-top jar. Season with salt and pepper, then stir into potatoes. Just before serving, sprinkle with chopped herbs and gently fold in. Garnish with sprigs of herbs.

Serves 4-6.

6 baking potatoes
vegetable oil
2 tablespoons white wine vinegar
1 bunch spring onions, finely sliced
1 egg yolk
pinch of dry mustard
salt and pepper
1 teaspoon sage leaves, finely chopped
155 ml (5 fl oz/⅔ cup) thick sour cream
fresh sage leaves, to garnish

Scrub potatoes and dry on absor-bent kitchen paper. Prick deeply through skins and rub with oil.

Wrap potatoes separately in double thickness foil and bake in coals for 45 minutes-1 hour, turn-ing occasionally until soft. Put vinegar in a small saucepan, add spring onions and cook over low heat until vinegar has almost evaporated. Remove pan from heat. Beat together egg yolk, mustard and salt and pepper to taste and stir into spring onions.

Cook over very low heat for 1 minute, beating continuously until mixture thickens. Care must be taken not to overheat or sauce may curdle. Remove from heat; stir in chopped sage and cream. Cut a deep cross through foil into cooked potatoes and squeeze sides to open out. Spoon in a little sauce. Garnish with sage leaves.

Serves 6.

GREEN LENTIL COURGETTES

3 large firm courgettes (zucchini)
2 spring onions
1 small green pepper (capsicum)
1 tomato
125 g (4 oz) cooked green lentils
1 teaspoon fresh basil leaves, snipped
salt and pepper
3 tablespoons grated, roasted hazelnuts
basil sprigs, to garnish

Halve courgettes (zucchini) length-wise. Scoop pulp into a bowl, leaving 0.5 cm (¼ in) thick shells to prevent courgettes (zucchini) from collapsing. Reserve shells.

Finely slice spring onions; core, seed and finely chop green pepper (capsicum); skin and chop tomato.

Add to the courgette (zucchini) pulp and mix in lentils and basil. Season to taste with salt and pepper. Pile mixture high into reserved shells.

Place the courgette (zucchini) halves individually on large squares of double thickness foil. Wrap up securely, leaving a space above the stuffing for steam to circulate. Barbecue on rack over hot coals for about 20 minutes until courgettes (zucchini) are tender, but firm. Open packets and sprinkle hazelnuts over stuffing. Garnish with sprigs of basil.

Serves 6.

CURRIED RICE SALAD

90 g (3 oz) semi-dried apricots, chopped
250 g (8 oz/1⅓ cups) long grain brown rice
3 tablespoons sunflower oil
60 g (2 oz/⅓ cup) cashew nuts
1 onion, chopped
1 teaspoon cumin seeds
3 teaspoons curry powder
90 ml (3 fl oz/⅓ cup) orange juice
60 g (2 oz/⅓ cup) raisins
salt and pepper
coriander sprigs, to garnish

Put chopped apricots in a bowl, pour over sufficient boiling water to cover and leave to soak for 45 minutes.

Meanwhile, cook rice in boiling salted water for 40 minutes until tender.

Heat the oil in a frying pan, add cashew nuts and fry until golden.

Remove with a slotted spoon and drain on absorbent kitchen paper. Add onion to pan and cook over a medium heat for 3-4 minutes. Stir in cumin seeds and curry powder and cook for 2 minutes. Pour in orange juice and simmer for 1 minute. Remove from heat.

Drain rice, rinse under cold running water, then drain again. Put into a large bowl, add the warm curry sauce and mix well.

Drain apricots and stir into rice with nuts and raisins. Season with salt and pepper. Allow the salad to stand for at least 2 hours before serving to allow flavours to mingle. Serve garnished with sprigs of fresh coriander.

Serves 6.

PINEAPPLE CREAM

AMARETTI MOUSSE

3 slices fresh pineapple
440 g (14 oz) can evaporated milk, well chilled
2 teaspoons powdered gelatine
juice of ½ lemon
caster sugar, to taste

TO DECORATE:

crystallized pineapple
crystallized angelica

Cut away all skin and 'eyes' from pineapple and cut out core. Purée the flesh in a blender or food processor.

In a bowl, whip evaporated milk until thick and creamy. Sprinkle gelatine over lemon juice in a small bowl and leave to soften for 2-3 minutes. Stand bowl in a saucepan of hot water and stir until the gelatine has dissolved. Stir it into the whipped milk.

Fold pineapple purée into whipped milk and sweeten to taste with sugar. Pour into a glass serving bowl or individual glasses and chill until set. Decorate with crystallized pineapple and angelica cut into leaf shapes just before serving.

Serves 4.

100 g (3½ oz/½ cup) whole blanched almonds
60 g (2 oz) amaretti biscuits
3 eggs, plus 2 extra yolks
90 g (3 oz/⅓ cup) caster sugar
3 teaspoons powdered gelatine
2 tablespoons lemon juice
1-2 tablespoons Amaretto or kirsch
315 ml (10 fl oz/1¼ cups) whipping cream

Toast nuts under a medium grill to brown. Put with biscuits in food processor fitted with metal blade and process to crumbs.

In a bowl, whisk eggs, extra yolks and sugar together until thick and mousse-like. Sprinkle gelatine over lemon juice in a small bowl and leave to soften for 2-3 minutes. Stand bowl in saucepan of hot water and stir until gelatine has dissolved. Add to egg mixture with liqueur and three-quarters of nut and biscuit mixture. Whip cream stiffly and fold two-thirds into mixture.

Pour mixture into a 1 litre (32 fl oz/ 4 cup) soufflé dish and put in refrigerator to set. Just before serving, decorate with piped rosettes of reserved whipping cream and sprinkle remaining nuts and biscuits on top.

Serves 6-8.

Note: Amaretto is a very sweet liqueur made from almonds. Kirsch gives a more subtle flavour and makes the dessert less sweet.

GRAND MARNIER KEBABS

TARTE FRANÇAISE

3 firm apricots
3 firm fresh figs
two 2.5 cm (1 in) thick trimmed pineapple slices
2 satsumas
2 firm bananas
2 eating apples
1 tablespoon lemon juice
90 g (3 oz/⅓ cup) unsalted butter
90 g (3 oz/½ cup) icing sugar
1 tablespoon Grand Marnier
1 tablespoon fresh orange juice
1 tablespoon finely grated orange peel

Halve apricots and remove stones. Remove stalks and quarter figs lengthwise.

Remove any woody core and cut pineapple slices into chunks. Peel satsumas and quarter but do not remove membranes. Peel bananas and cut into 2.5 cm (1 in) thick slices. Peel apples, cut into quarters, remove cores and halve each apple piece crosswise. Sprinkle apples and bananas with lemon juice to prevent discoloration.

Thread fruit onto 6-8 skewers, making sure that each has a mixture of fruit and starting and finishing with apple and pineapple. Melt butter, stir in icing sugar, then add Grand Marnier, orange juice and peel. Brush kebabs with sauce and barbecue over medium coals for 5-6 minutes, frequently basting with sauce. Serve any remaining sauce with kebabs. Serve hot.

Serves 6-8.

410 g (13 oz) puff pastry, thawed if frozen
1 egg yolk, beaten
6 tablespoons apricot jam, sieved
2 tablespoons lemon juice
about 750 g (1½ lb) mixed fresh fruit, such as grapes, strawberries and/or raspberries and bananas

Preheat oven to 220C (425F/Gas 7). Roll out pastry to a 30 x 20 cm (12 x 8 in) rectangle. Fold pastry in half, to a 15 x 20 cm (6 x 8 in) rectangle. Cut a rectangle from folded edge, 4 cm (1½ in) in from outside edges.

Unfold middle section and roll out to same size as 'frame' – 30 x 20 cm (12 x 8 in). Place on a baking sheet, dampen edges with water, then unfold 'frame' and place carefully on top of pastry rectangle. Press edges of pastry together, then 'knock up' using a blunt knife. Mark a pattern on frame and brush with beaten egg yolk. Prick centre of case all over.

Leave pastry in a cool place for 10 minutes, then bake for about 20 minutes, until golden brown. Leave to cool. Put jam and lemon juice into a saucepan and heat gently until jam has melted. To prepare fruit, halve and seed grapes, leave strawberries and/or raspberries whole and peel and slice bananas. Brush base of tart lightly with jam and arrange fruit in rows. Brush fruit with jam and serve as soon as possible.

Serves 6.

COCKTAIL PARTIES

Cocktail parties are versatile and convenient. They are an excellent way of entertaining a large number of people at once, and they can be either formal or informal. They also require less preparation and are much easier to manage than parties involving both a meal and drinks.

SETTING THE ROOM

Set up a number of small tables and a few chairs around the room. Do not make the mistake of creating a buffet; guests will end up with a drink in one hand, a plate in the other, nowhere to sit and without a free hand to eat anything anyway! Your guests should not need plates, but a good supply of paper napkins is useful for messy fingers.

Aim to spread the food around the room on the small tables. If possible, keep some plates of food circulating. As host or hostess, this is a good opportunity for you to keep circulating too. Although children are usually excluded from cocktail parties, you may find that they can be of great service by offering trays of finger-food to guests. Remember to lay out a number of ashtrays, not just for smokers but also useful for olive stones, cocktail sticks or discarded canapés.

THE COCKTAILS

When planning a cocktail party, offer a limited choice of drinks – no one expects you to stock the entire contents of a commercial bar – but make sure your selection is creative. Concentrate your choice around two or three basic spirits, such as gin, vodka and whisky, and several other ingredients, such as vermouth (dry and sweet), creme de cacao, and Cointreau. In addition to these, you will need non-alcoholic mixers: tomato, orange and pineapple juice, soda and tonic water, and fizzy drinks such as lemonade and ginger ale. Garnishes are important to many cocktails so be sure to stock such items as lemons, limes, olives, slices of fruit, powdered sugar and cherries. Make a point to include non-alcoholic punches and fruit-based drinks for those guests who are driving or do not drink alcohol (see pages 50-51).

The cocktail recipes in this book are based on measures (msrs.). A standard measure is equivalent to one-sixth of a gill, which is slightly less than one fluid ounce or 25-30 millilitres. A 'dash' is simply the quantity released in a quick spurt from a bottle. As a cocktail is defined as a drink composed of at least two ingredients which have been shaken or stirred together, the term can cover a vast array of beverages. Cocktails can be as exotic or as straightforward as you like.

For preparing cocktails, use either a blender, shaker or mixing glass (see clockwise). The strainer is used when pouring drinks from the shaker to the glass to hold back ice and fruit. Other equipment includes a measure, chopping board, long-handled spoon, melon-baller, canelle knife, paring knife and decorative cutters (for garnishes).

BITE-SIZED SAVOURIES

Apart from crisps and peanuts, your guests will expect a few snacks to accompany their cocktails, and this is where you can excel. Unlike a dinner party, virtually all the dishes on the following pages can be prepared well in advance, sealed in plastic wrap and stored in the refrigerator or in airtight containers. If they need to be served hot, it is just a matter of heating them in the oven.

All these recipes are bite-sized and easy to eat with one hand. They are also savoury rather than sweet. Unless you really have strong feelings on the subject, stick to savoury foods; they are far more complementary to cocktail drinking.

Twist whole or half slices of citrus fruit together with a cherry or pineapple leaf; secure with a cocktail stick.

Half slices of pineapple may be used to garnish tropical cocktails. Decorate slice with a cherry and three pineapple leaves.

Cut a slice from a small, dark green-skinned watermelon. Make an incision to balance slice on glass. Add cherry.

Replace the green leaf of a strawberry with a sprig of mint. Secure with a cocktail stick. Slice berry to balance on glass.

SPICED CRACKED OLIVES

DEVILLED MIXED NUTS

1 kg (2 lb) large green olives
2 or 3 red chillies
4 cloves garlic, peeled
3 sprigs each fresh dill, thyme and oregano
2 teaspoons fennel seeds
olive oil to cover

Make a lengthwise slit in each olive, cutting in as far as the stone. (This allows flavours to penetrate.)

Put olives into a jar with the chillies, garlic, dill, thyme, oregano and fennel seeds. Pour in oil to cover and store, covered in the refrigerator, for several days or weeks. Drain and serve as an appetizer with drinks or in salads. More olives can be added to the oil,

or the oil may be used afterwards for cooking or in salads.

Makes 1 kg (2 lb).

CALAMATTA OLIVES WITH GARLIC
Put calamatta olives (a variety of Greek olive with distinctive flavour), with peeled cloves of garlic in a jar and pour in olive oil or a mixture of olive and vegetable oil. Cover and store in the refrigerator for a few days or several weeks. Drain and serve. The oil may be used for cooking and salad dressings. A few whole chillies may be added to give bite.

125 g (4 oz) almonds
45 g (1½ oz) butter
2 cloves garlic, crushed
1 teaspoon Worcestershire sauce
2 teaspoons curry powder
pinch of cayenne
125 g (4 oz) raw cashew nuts
125 g (4 oz) pecan nuts
chilli flower, to garnish (optional)

Blanch the almonds by pouring boiling water over the nuts and leaving a few minutes. Lift the nuts out and they will slip out of their skins easily.

Melt the butter and stir in the garlic, Worcestershire sauce, curry powder and cayenne. Sprinkle evenly over all the nuts in an oven-proof dish and toss well to coat.

Cook at 180C (350F/Gas 4) for 15 to 20 minutes, stirring every 5 minutes to colour evenly. Remove nuts from the oven and cool. Store in an airtight container until ready to serve with drinks. Serve in a bowl and garnish with a chilli flower, if desired.

Serves 4-6.

CHEESE THINS

125 g (4 oz/1 cup) plain flour
½ teaspoon salt
½ teaspoon pepper
½ teaspoon dry mustard
125 g (4 oz/½ cup) butter
125 g (4 oz/1 cup) grated Cheddar cheese
4 teaspoons fine oatmeal
1 teaspoon cayenne pepper
1 egg white

Preheat oven to 220C (425F/Gas 7). Lightly butter 2 baking sheets. Sift flour, salt, pepper and mustard into a bowl. Cut butter into pieces, add to bowl and rub in finely until mixture begins to cling together.

Using a fork, stir in cheese and mix to a soft dough. Knead on a lightly floured surface and roll out very thinly. Using a 2.5 cm (1 in) oval cutter, cut out 80 oval shapes. Arrange on baking sheets, spaced well apart.

Mix together oatmeal and cayenne. Brush each oval with egg white and sprinkle with oatmeal mixture. Bake in the oven for 5-6 minutes until pale in colour. Cool on baking sheets, then remove carefully with a palette knife.

Makes 80.

CARAWAY PRETZELS

185 g (6 oz/1½ cups) plain flour
½ teaspoon baking powder
½ teaspoon salt
90 g (3 oz/⅓ cup) butter
3 teaspoons caraway seeds
60 ml (2 fl oz/¼ cup) boiling water
1 egg white, very lightly beaten

Preheat oven to 180C (350F/Gas 4). Butter several baking sheets. Sift flour, baking powder and salt into a bowl. Rub in butter until mixture resembles fine bread-crumbs, then mix in 1 teaspoon of caraway seeds. Add boiling water and mix to form a soft dough.

Knead dough lightly on a floured surface until smooth. Divide into 36 equal pieces, about 7 g (¼ oz) each. Take one piece of dough and shape into a long thin strand, about 35 cm (14 in) long. Bring ends round to form a loop; cross over, then take back up to top of loop. Press firmly in position to secure. Place on a baking sheet. Repeat with remaining pieces of dough.

Brush pretzels with egg white and sprinkle evenly with remaining caraway seeds. Bake in the oven for 18-20 minutes until lightly browned. Carefully remove from baking sheets to wire racks to cool.

Makes 36.

MUSHROOM KNAPSACKS

VEGETABLE CURRY ENVELOPES

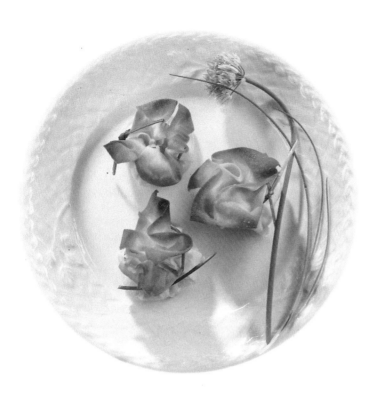

4 sheets filo pastry
45 g (1½ oz/9 teaspoons) butter, melted
250 g (8 oz) button mushrooms
82 g (2¾ oz) Boursin cheese
chives, to garnish

Preheat the oven to 220C (425F/ Gas 7). Brush 2 sheets of filo pastry with butter and lay the other 2 sheets of pastry on top of them. Cut each double sheet into about twelve 7.5 cm (3 in) squares.

Remove stalks from mushrooms and fill cavities with ¼ teaspoon-fuls of Boursin cheese. Put each mushroom, cheese side up, into the centre of a square of pastry and bring up the edges to enclose the mushroom completely, leaving the pastry edges pointing upwards.

Brush tops of pastry with butter and bake in the oven for 5 minutes until crisp and golden. Remove them from the oven and allow to cool slightly.

Tie a single chive around the top of each bundle and serve them while still warm.

Makes about 24.

60 g (2 oz) puff pastry, thawed
1 egg, beaten
1 teaspoon cumin seeds

FILLING:
15 g (½ oz/3 teaspoons) butter
1 leek, finely chopped
1 clove garlic, crushed
1 teaspoon ground cumin
1 teaspoon garam masala
2 teaspoons mango chutney
½ teaspoon finely grated lime peel
2 teaspoons lime juice
60 g (2 oz) cooked, diced potato

Melt butter for the curry filling in a small saucepan. Add leek and garlic to pan.

Cook quickly for 1 minute, stirring. Add cumin, garam masala, chutney, lime peel and juice. Stir well, cook gently for 1-2 minutes, then add potatoes, mix well and cool. Preheat oven to 220C (425F/ Gas 7).Roll out puff pastry very thinly to an oblong measuring 30 × 20 cm (12 × 8 in). Cut into twenty-four 5 cm (2 in) squares. Brush edges with beaten egg and place a little filling in centre of each.

Draw all corners to centre and seal joins to form a tiny envelope. Repeat to seal all pastry envelopes. Arrange on a baking sheet, brush with egg to glaze and sprinkle with cumin seeds. Cook in the oven for 5-8 minutes until well risen and golden brown.

Makes 24.

TARAMASALATA TOASTS

8 thin slices brown or white bread

45 g (1½ oz/9 teaspoons) butter, softened

2 tablespoons sesame seeds

185-250 g (6-8 oz) taramasalata

4 stoned black olives, cut into slivers, and tiny parsley sprigs, to garnish

Toast slices of bread until lightly golden. Leave to cool, standing upright.

Using a 5 cm (2 in) star-shaped biscuit cutter, cut out 8 shapes from toast. Spread shapes with butter.

Toast sesame seeds until lightly golden and leave to cool. Sprinkle sesame seeds over shapes, shaking off excess.

Put taramasalata into a piping bag fitted with a large star nozzle. Pipe a generous rosette of mixture onto each star.

Garnish each one with thin slivers of black olives and parsley.

Makes 8.

Variation: Replace taramasalata with softened cream cheese and sprinkle toast with finely chopped chives instead of sesame seeds.

ANCHOVY MOSAICS

60 g (2 oz/¼ cup) butter, softened

1¼ teaspoons lemon juice

half 50 g (2 oz) can anchovy fillets, drained and very finely chopped

1 cocktail gherkin, finely chopped

1 teaspoon capers, well drained and finely chopped

½-1 teaspoon finely chopped fresh marjoram

½ teaspoon thousand island dressing

2 large thin slices brown bread

2 large thin slices white bread

2-3 slices peeled avocado, about 0.5 cm (¼ in) thick

1 canned pimento cap, well drained and patted dry

marjoram sprigs, to garnish

In a bowl, mix together 30 g (1 oz/6 teaspoons) butter, ¼ teaspoon lemon juice, anchovies, gherkin, capers, marjoram and dressing.

Spread mixture over brown bread slices. Using a 5 cm (2 in) fluted round biscuit cutter, cut out 4 rounds from each slice to make 8 pieces in total.

Spread remaining plain butter over white bread and, using same cutter, cut out 4 rounds from each slice to make 8 in total.

Using a small star-shaped cutter, measuring about 2.5 cm (1 in), cut out centres from each white bread round and discard. Place star-shaped rounds of bread, buttered sides down, over brown bread rounds and press lightly together to form 8 sandwiches.

Dip slices of avocado in remaining lemon juice and, using the star cutter, cut out 4 stars. Cut out 4 stars from pimento. Place avocado and pimento stars into shapes in white bread. Garnish with sprigs of marjoram.

Makes 8.

HOT PRAWN FRIES

4 large medium-thick slices white bread, crusts removed
15 g (½ oz/3 teaspoons) butter, softened
15 g (½ oz/6 teaspoons) plain flour
75 ml (2½ fl oz/⅓ cup) milk
2 teaspoons grated Parmesan cheese
finely grated rind of ½ lemon
90 g (3 oz) peeled cooked prawns, thawed if frozen and chopped
1 tablespoon chopped fresh parsley
salt and pepper
vegetable oil for deep frying
1 egg, beaten
3 tablespoons dry breadcrumbs
peeled cooked prawns and small slices of lemon and dill sprigs, to garnish

Using a rolling pin, firmly roll each slice of bread to flatten. Melt butter in a saucepan. Stir in flour and cook for 1 minute, then stir in milk and bring to the boil, stirring. Simmer for 2 minutes, stirring constantly.

Remove from heat and stir in cheese, lemon rind, prawns and parsley. Season with salt and pepper.

Spread slices of bread with sauce. Roll up like a Swiss roll and cut each roll into 5 slices.

Half-fill a deep-fat fryer or pan with oil and heat to 190C (375F) or until a cube of day-old bread browns in 40 seconds.

Meanwhile, dip each roll in beaten egg and coat in bread-crumbs. Fry in hot oil until golden. Drain on absorbent kitchen paper.

Serve hot on cocktail sticks, skewered with prawns, lemon slices and dill.

Makes 20.

AVOCADO SALMON ROLLS

90 g (3 oz) sliced smoked salmon
3 slices rye bread
30 g (1 oz/3 teaspoons) butter
dill sprigs and lemon twists, to garnish

FILLING:

60 g (2 oz/¼ cup) full fat soft cheese
½ avocado, mashed
2 teaspoons chopped fresh dill
1 small tomato, skinned, seeded and chopped
¼ teaspoon ground black pepper

To make filling, put cheese in a bowl and beat until soft. Add avocado and stir until blended.

Add dill, chopped tomato and pepper and stir gently. Place in a piping bag fitted with 1 cm (½ in) plain nozzle. Cut smoked salmon into 20 oblongs measuring about 4 × 2.5 cm (1½ × 1 in). Pipe a length of cheese mixture across top of a short edge of each salmon oblong. Roll up each one neatly.

Spread rye bread with butter, then cut into 20 rectangles to fit salmon rolls. Place a salmon roll on each piece and garnish with sprigs of dill and lemon twists.

Makes 20.

CHICKEN LIVER SIZZLES

| 3 rashers streaky bacon, rinded |
| 3 chicken livers, thawed if frozen and halved |
| 3 large medium-thick slices white bread, crusts removed |
| 30 g (1 oz/6 teaspoons) butter, softened |
| Dijon mustard, to taste |
| 3 slices processed Cheddar cheese |
| salt and pepper |
| a little corn oil for brushing |
| 6 cherry tomatoes, halved, and watercress sprigs, to garnish |

Preheat oven to 190C (375F/Gas 5). Stretch bacon rashers on a board using the back of a knife, until doubled in length. Cut each rasher in half. Pat chicken livers dry on absorbent kitchen paper.

Using a rolling pin, firmly roll slices of bread to flatten. Spread one side of each slice with butter and then mustard, to taste.

Cover each slice of bread with a slice of cheese, then cut each one in half lengthwise. Add a chicken liver to each one and season with salt and pepper.

Roll up slices of bread firmly. Wrap a bacon rasher around each one and secure with 2 cocktail sticks. Cut in half between cocktail sticks to make 12 portions.

Place on a greased baking sheet and brush lightly with oil. Cook for 12-15 minutes or until cooked and golden. Replace cocktail sticks with new ones. Thread half a tomato onto each stick and serve hot, garnished with watercress.

Makes 12.

GLAZED CHICKEN CANAPÉS

| 90 g (3 oz/⅓ cup) butter |
| 30 g (1 oz/9 teaspoons) plain flour |
| 315 ml (10 fl oz/1¼ cups) milk |
| salt and white pepper |
| 24 g (0.85 oz) packet aspic jelly powder |
| 4-6 slices skinned cooked chicken breast (fillet), about 0.5 cm (¼ in) thick |
| 1 cap canned pimento, drained |
| a little cucumber skin |
| a few parsley stalks |
| 8 slices pumpernickel |
| 60 g (2 oz/½ cup) pistachio nuts, chopped, and chervil sprigs, to garnish |

Melt 30 g (1 oz/6 teaspoons) butter in a saucepan. Stir in flour and cook for 1 minute. Stir in milk and bring to the boil, stirring. Simmer for 2 minutes, stirring until thickened. Season with salt and pepper.

Make up aspic according to packet instructions, but use only 315 ml (10 fl oz/1¼ cups) boiling water. Stir half the warm aspic into warm sauce then sieve.

Cut chicken into 15-20 rounds, using a 4 cm (1½ in) plain cutter. Place on a wire rack over a plate. Coat with sauce, allowing excess to run off. Leave to set for 15 minutes.

Dry pimento and cut into flowers, using aspic cutters. Cut cucumber skin into leaf shapes and parsley stalks into neat stems. Dip decorations into remaining aspic, then arrange on chicken to form 'flowers'. Leave for 15 minutes.

Spoon aspic over shapes to glaze. Leave to set for 30 minutes. Using same cutter as before, cut pumpernickel into 15-20 rounds. Spread tops and edges with butter and dip edges in nuts. Place chicken rounds on bread and garnish with chervil.

Makes 15-20.

QUAIL'S EGG SPECIALS

6 quail's eggs

3 large slices white or brown bread

90 g (3 oz/⅓ cup) butter, softened

½ teaspoon lemon juice

3 good pinches cayenne pepper

3 slices Sage Derby cheese, about 0.3 cm (⅛ in) thick

1 kiwi fruit, peeled

finely shredded sage leaves, to garnish

Put quail's eggs into a saucepan of boiling water and simmer gently for 4 minutes. Drain and cover at once with cold water. Shell eggs and keep in a bowl of cold water until required. Drain and pat dry before using.

Toast slices of bread. Using a 5 cm (2 in) fluted round biscuit cutter, cut out 6 rounds and leave to cool, standing upright.

In a bowl, mix butter with lemon juice and cayenne pepper. Spread a little butter over toast rounds. Put remaining butter in a small grease-proof paper piping bag fitted with a small star nozzle.

Using the same cutter, cut out 3 rounds of cheese. Cut cheese rounds into quarters and arrange 2 on toast rounds, at opposite sides with pointed ends inwards.

Cut three 0.3 cm (⅛ in) thick slices of kiwi fruit and cut into quarters. Arrange 2 quarters between cheese on toast rounds.

Pipe a neat rosette of flavoured butter in centre and place a quail's egg on top. Scatter eggs with sage.

Makes 6.

Variation: Use any type of cheese you prefer, although choosing one with an attractive 'veining' (blue, red or green) gives added interest.

EGG TAPENADE

6 hard-boiled eggs

18 black olives

5 canned anchovy fillets, drained

1 tablespoon drained capers

100 g (3½ oz) canned tuna, drained

3 tablespoons olive oil

lemon juice, to taste

fresh parsley leaves to garnish

Shell the eggs and halve crosswise using a stainless steel knife. Remove the yolks and trim bases so eggs stand upright.

Reserve 6 olives for garnish. Cut the flesh away from the remaining olives and discard the stones. Put the olive flesh, anchovies, capers, egg yolks and drained tuna into the bowl of a food processor. Blend together, gradually adding the oil to make a thick purée. Season with lemon juice. Chill.

Spoon egg yolk mixture into the white halves. Slice reserved olives in half and place a slice on top of each egg. Garnish with parsley leaves. The eggs can be hard-boiled and prepared up to 2 days before serving. Keep whites in a bowl, with water to cover and refrigerate.

Makes 12.

MARTINI (dry)

MANHATTAN (dry)

ice cubes	
2½ msrs. dry gin	
½ msr. dry vermouth	
olive and knot of lemon peel	

Fill Martini pitcher with ice. Gently pour in gin. Add vermouth and stir gently. Strain into chilled Martini glass and add olive and knot of lemon peel.

ice cubes	
1½ msrs. Canadian whisky	
¾ msr. dry vermouth	
1 or 2 dashes Angostura bitters	
1 olive	
knot of lemon peel	

Stir ice with whisky, vermouth and bitters. Strain into Martini glass. Spear olive with cocktail pick and balance on edge of glass. Add knot of lemon peel.

CUBA LIBRE

ZOMBIE

1 msr. light rum
juice of ½ lime
ice cubes
cola
slice of lime

Pour rum and lime into an ice filled highball glass and stir well. Fill with cola. Garnish with slice of lime and serve with a straw.

cracked ice
1 msr. dark rum
1 msr. Jamaican rum
1 msr. light rum
1 msr. lemon or lime juice
4 dashes passion fruit or orange juice
4 dashes apricot brandy
4 dashes cherry brandy
fresh fruit, such as pineapple, kiwi fruit, papaya or paw paw, cherries, to garnish

Half fill blender with cracked ice. Add dark rum, Jamaican rum, light rum, lemon or lime juice, passion fruit or orange juice, apricot brandy and cherry brandy and blend well. Pour into large glass. Garnish with fruit and serve with straws.

CHI CHI

cracked ice
1½ msrs. vodka
1 msr. coconut cream
4 msrs. unsweetened pineapple juice
1 maraschino cherry
slice of pineapple
2 pineapple leaves

Place cracked ice in blender. Add vodka, coconut cream and pineapple juice. Blend for 10 seconds — any longer will dilute drink. Strain into large glass. Garnish with cherry, slice of pineapple and leaves. Serve with a straw.

SCREWDRIVER

1½ msrs. vodka
2 ice cubes
orange juice
1 maraschino cherry
slice of orange

Pour vodka over ice cubes in highball glass. Fill with orange juice. Garnish with cherry and slice of orange. Serve with a straw.

PINA COLADA

cracked ice
1 ½ msrs. light rum
1 msr. pineapple juice
1 msr. coconut milk
½ msr. cream
1 maraschino cherry
piece of pineapple
1 hollowed-out coconut, if desired

Combine ice with rum, pineapple juice, coconut milk and cream in shaker. Shake until frosty. Strain into a hollowed-out coconut, if desired, or large glass. Garnish with cherry and pineapple slice. Serve with a straw.

RAMOZ FIZZ

lemon wedge
caster sugar
cracked ice
2 msrs. dry gin
1 msr. fresh lemon juice
1 msr. fresh lime juice
1 msr. whipping cream
2 dashes orange flower water
1 teaspoon sugar
1 egg white
soda water
1 orchid, if desired

Frost the rim of highball glass with lemon and sugar. Shake cracked ice with remaining ingredients except soda water. Strain into glass, top with soda water and stir gently. Garnish with an orchid, if desired.

ROSY PIPPIN

LIME & MINT SHERBERT

4-6 limes
60 g (2 oz/¼ cup) caster sugar
pinch of salt
handful mint leaves
ice cubes
about 1 litre (32 fl oz/4 cups) iced water
mint leaves and lime slices, to decorate

Squeeze enough limes to make 90 ml (3 fl oz/⅓ cup) juice.

Put the juice in a blender or food processor fitted with a metal blade. Add sugar, salt and mint leaves and process until smooth. Strain into a jug, then chill.

Half-fill tall glasses with ice cubes, add a little lime juice concentrate and top up with iced water. Serve at once, decorated with mint leaves and lime slices.

Makes about 1.2 litres (2 pints/ 5 cups).

1 dash Grenadine
1 dash lemon juice
¼ cup/4 msrs. apple juice
ginger ale
slice of apple

Add Grenadine and lemon juice to apple juice and stir well. Pour into glass. Fill with ginger ale. Garnish with slice of apple.

POND PUNCH

ROSE PETAL INFUSION

250 ml (8 fl oz/1 cup) pineapple juice

250 ml (8 fl oz/1 cup) grapefruit juice

juice of 1 lemon

500 ml (16 fl oz/2 cups) sparkling
mineral water

2-4 teaspoons canned mint syrup

ice cubes

pineapple chunks

mint sprigs and pineapple wedges,
to garnish

Mix together the fruit juices,
sparkling mineral water and canned
mint syrup. Fill tall glasses with
large ice cubes and pineapple
chunks. Pour over the punch and
garnish with sprigs of mint and
wedges of pineapple.

Serves 4-6.

3 rosehips teabags

315 ml (10 fl oz/1 ¼ cups) boiling water

6-9 teaspoons rosehip syrup

handful scented rose petals

9 teaspoons triple distilled rosewater

625 ml (20 fl oz/2 ½ cups) sparkling
mineral water

ice cubes

rose petals, to decorate

Put teabags into a bowl and pour
over the boiling water. Leave to
infuse for 10 minutes, then remove
teabags and leave liquid to cool.

When completely cold, stir in
rosehip syrup, rose petals and rosewater and leave to infuse for a
further 30 minutes. Strain and add
mineral water.

Fill tall glasses with ice cubes,
pour over the rose petal infusion
and decorate with petals.

Serves 4-6.

DINNER PARTIES

Dinner parties are usually formal affairs. Thought, preparation and care as well as good timing are necessary for a successful evening. However, do not feel as if you must adhere to strict rules of dinner etiquette. Depending on the guests you invite and the atmosphere you want to convey, you may want your party to be slightly less formal. In either case, your party will be a unique and individual experience for your guests because your particular style will pervade.

PREPARATION

If you are holding a dinner party for the first time, try not to be too ambitious. Cater for a maximum of eight people (including yourself). Most recipes on the following pages are designed for four people, so you will only need to double the ingredients given. Also, try out any new dishes a week or two beforehand. This will give you time to work out any problems that arise with the recipe and it will give you more confidence for the real event. It may also give you an opportunity to discover some short-cuts to save yourself valuable time. Remember that family members are usually eager to sample any test dishes and they may offer helpful suggestions.

Write out your menu and work out the preparation and cooking times so they flow smoothly. Remember to allow time to prepare yourself for the party. Try to ensure that at least one course (usually the appetizer or dessert) is prepared the day before and refrigerated.

Select good quality fresh ingredients whenever possible. The better the basics, the better the chance is for a perfect result. Do not leave your shopping too late or expect your local supermarket to stock all the items you will need. You want to avoid any last-minute panic.

Prepare cutlery, crockery, glasses and table linen at least a day in advance. Make sure you have the proper quantity and that they are spotlessly clean. Plan a simple but attractive table setting (refer to pages 6-7 for tips on preparation).

FOOD & DRINK

The recipes on the following pages are appetizing and sophisticated without being difficult to prepare. Among the appetizers, side dishes, main courses and desserts suggested here, choose dishes that complement each other visually as well as in taste and texture.

Right: This diagram shows the seating arrangement for a formal dinner. The host and hostess sit at opposite ends of the table, the host with the female guest of honour to his right and the hostess with the male guest of honour to her right. Couples do not sit together but are placed diagonally opposite each other. The seating arrangement is as follows:
A) Host; B) Female; C) Male;
D) Female; E) Male guest of honour; F) Hostess; G) Male; H) Female; I) Male; J) Female guest of honour.

Left: Frosted fruit (fruit coated with egg white and powdered sugar) makes a table setting look stunning. Candles, flowers and napkin folds can all add that special touch to the evening.

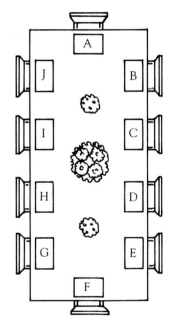

Keep your menu balanced and uncluttered. Three courses is perfectly adequate, followed by coffee and chocolates or fresh fruit. Cheese can be served either before dessert (in the French fashion) or afterwards with a glass of port or sweet dessert wine. Try to balance the dishes; if one course is rich and substantial, keep the others light.

For a formal affair, offer an aperitif before dinner, then chilled white wine with the appetizer, and either red or white wine with the main course. Traditionally, red wine is served with red meat and white wine with white meat; however, this is no longer always essential. Many light, young red wines can be served chilled and are ideal with veal, pork or chicken. Remember to chill the white wine for at least two hours in advance, but not the day before or it can become tasteless. Let full-bodied red wine breathe – open it at least one hour before the meal, letting it reach room temperature. In addition, be sure to stock plenty of mineral water and a small selection of other non-alcoholic drinks.

If in doubt, simplify. This will allow you more time with your guests, and will more likely result in a successful and satisfying dinner party.

NECTARINES & PROSCIUTTO

mixed salad leaves	
2 nectarines or peaches	
125 g (4 oz) prosciutto (cured ham)	
fresh raspberries, to garnish, if desired	

RASPBERRY VINAIGRETTE:	
3 tablespoons virgin olive oil	
5 teaspoons sunflower oil	
3 teaspoons raspberry vinegar	

Divide salad leaves between 4 plates.

Slice nectarines, halve slices of prosciutto (cured ham) and wrap around the fruit. Arrange on the salad leaves.

To make the dressing, mix ingredients together in a bowl or screw-top jar. Drizzle over the salad, then serve garnished with fresh raspberries, if desired.

Serves 4 as a starter.

MELON & TOMATO SALAD

1 small honeydew melon or 2 galia, cantaloupe or rock melons	
375 g (12 oz) tomatoes, skinned	
mint sprigs, to garnish	

MINT DRESSING:	
2 tablespoons sunflower oil	
2 teaspoons sherry vinegar	
1 tablespoon chopped fresh mint	
pepper	

Cut melon or melons in half, remove seeds, then cut the flesh into cubes (or balls using a melon scoop) and place in a bowl.

Quarter the tomatoes, remove seeds and cut each wedge across into 4 pieces. Add to the melon.

To make the dressing, mix all the ingredients together in a bowl or screw-top jar. Pour over the salad and stir gently. Cover well and chill for flavours to mingle.

Remove from refrigerator 30 minutes before serving. Spoon into 4 dishes or, if using the smaller variety of melons, spoon salad into the shells. Serve garnished with sprigs of mint.

Serves 4 as a starter.

LIVER-PISTACHIO PÂTÉ

MARINATED ARTICHOKES

250 g (8 oz) chicken livers
125 g (4 oz) butter
1 small onion, chopped
1 clove garlic, chopped
2 tablespoons Cognac or brandy
2 tablespoons single cream
90 g (3 oz/½ cup) whole pistachio nuts
extra 2-3 tablespoons melted butter and
extra pistachio nuts, to garnish
Melba toast, to serve

Carefully pick over the livers, discarding any dark spots or green particles. Simmer livers in 500 ml (16 fl oz/2 cups) water for 5 minutes. Drain. Melt half the butter and gently sauté the onion and garlic without browning. Add the drained livers. Sauté until they are cooked through, stirring constantly. Cool.

Blend the livers until smooth in a food processor. Melt the remaining butter. Add butter, Cognac and cream to the liver mixture. Stir in the nuts.

Pour mixture into 6 to 8 individual ramekins and chill. Pour a thin layer of melted butter over each, sprinkle with more nuts and chill again. Serve with Melba toast.

Makes 6-8 ramekins.

400 g (14 oz) can artichoke hearts
6 tablespoons olive or vegetable oil
pepper
3 tablespoons chopped fresh mixed herbs
salt
juice of ½ lemon
red chilli slivers (optional)
1 clove garlic, crushed (optional)

Drain the artichokes and rinse well under cold running water to remove all the brine. Drain again and cut into halves or quarters.

Place the artichokes in a bowl, add the oil, a good grinding of pepper and the herbs. Mix together well, cover and refrigerate until ready to serve. Toss again before serving and add a squeeze of lemon juice and salt to taste.

For a bite, some slivers of fresh red chilli may be added to the artichokes; for garlic lovers, add a crushed garlic clove before chilling. The artichokes may be stored in a jar for up to 2 weeks, provided they are covered with the oil. Serve at room temperature. They may also be served on a croûton or added to salads.

Serves 4-6 as a starter.

LOBSTER & ASPARAGUS SALAD

CAVIAR MOUSSE

1 cooked lobster, weighing about 750 g (1½ lb)
250 g (8 oz) fresh asparagus, cut into 5 cm (2 in) pieces
heart of 1 spring cabbage, weighing about 185 g (6 oz), shredded
tarragon sprigs, to garnish

TARRAGON DRESSING:
3 tablespoons virgin olive oil
3 teaspoons tarragon vinegar
2 teaspoons chopped fresh tarragon, if desired
salt and pepper

To prepare lobster, remove large claws and pincers. Crack open claws; remove meat, trying to keep it in chunks. Using point of a sharp knife, split lobster into 2 pieces from head to tail. Starting at tail, remove meat, discarding brown feathery gills. Remove liver to use in another recipe. Remove dark coral if there is any and reserve. Extract meat from body with a skewer. Slice the tail meat.

Cook asparagus in a steamer for 7 minutes. Add cabbage and steam for a further 2 minutes. Arrange vegetables and lobster meat on 4 plates.

To make the dressing, mix all the ingredients in a bowl or screw-top jar, then drizzle over the salads. Garnish with lobster coral and sprigs of tarragon. Serve at once.

Serves 4 as a starter.

250 g (8 oz) black caviar
2 teaspoons gelatine
125 ml (4 fl oz/½ cup) boiling water
300 ml (10 fl oz) carton thick sour cream
3 spring onions, finely chopped
hard-boiled eggs and fresh herbs (optional), to garnish

The caviar mousse is best not made more than 24 hours before serving. Put the caviar in a bowl. Dissolve the gelatine in the boiling water and stir into the caviar.

Divide the caviar mixture between four small moulds or pour into one large mould. Chill until set. Meanwhile, combine the sour cream with the spring onions. Cover and chill until needed.

Unmould the caviar shapes by dipping the moulds into hot water and turning upside down on to a serving platter. Garnish with cut-out shapes of hard-boiled egg whites, sieved yolks, and sprigs of fresh herbs. Serve with the sour cream sauce and lemon wedges.

Makes 4 small moulds or 1 large mould.

SOLE WITH DILL STUFFING

four 185 g (6 oz) sole fillets, skinned
3 teaspoons lemon juice
salt and pepper
2 tablespoons vegetable oil
1 clove garlic, crushed
2.5 cm (1 in) piece fresh root ginger, grated
¼ teaspoon cayenne pepper
¼ teaspoon turmeric
4 spring onions, finely chopped
8 tablespoons finely chopped fresh dill
dill sprigs, to garnish

Wash fish fillets and pat dry with absorbent kitchen paper.

Lay fillets skinned-side up on work surface and sprinkle with lemon juice and salt and pepper, then set aside. Preheat oven to 180C (350F/Gas 4). Heat 1½ tablespoons oil in a frying pan. Add garlic, ginger, cayenne, turmeric and spring onions and cook over a low heat for 3 minutes or until onions are soft and golden, stirring occasionally. Remove from heat and set aside to cool, then stir in dill.

Divide stuffing between fillets and spread evenly over skinned side of fish. Roll fillets up from thickest end. Grease a shallow ovenproof dish with remaining oil and arrange sole rolls, seam-side down, in the dish with 60 ml (2 fl oz/¼ cup) water. Cover with foil and cook for 15-20 minutes or until fish flakes easily. Serve hot, with cooking juices spooned over and garnished with sprigs of dill.

Serves 4.

FISH IN HOT SAUCE

four 250 g (8 oz) whole fish, such as mackerel, trout, grey mullet or blue fish, cleaned
4 dill sprigs
4 lime slices
60 ml (2 fl oz/¼ cup) vegetable oil
4 spring onions, sliced
1 cm (½ in) piece fresh root ginger, grated
1 clove garlic, crushed
1 teaspoon mustard seeds
¼ teaspoon cayenne pepper
3 teaspoons tamarind paste
6 teaspoons tomato purée (paste)
dill sprigs and lime slices, to garnish

Wash fish and pat dry with absorbent kitchen paper. Slash 2 or 3 times on each side, tuck a sprig of dill and a lime slice inside each fish, then set aside.

Heat 2 tablespoons of oil in a small pan. Add onions and cook, stirring, for 2-3 minutes, until softened. Add ginger, garlic and mustard seeds and fry for 1 minute more, until mustard seeds start to pop.

Stir in cayenne pepper, tamarind paste, tomato purée (paste) and 90 ml (3 fl oz/⅓ cup) water. Bring to boil and simmer, uncovered, for about 5 minutes, until thickened slightly.

Meanwhile, heat grill. Place fish on grill rack, brush with remaining oil and cook for about 5 minutes on each side, basting occasionally with oil, until flesh flakes easily. Serve hot with the sauce, garnished with dill and lime slices.

Serves 4.

BARBECUED TROUT IN LEAVES

SALMON IN FILO PASTRY

4 trout or 8 small red mullet, cleaned	
8 vine leaves	
1 teaspoon arrowroot	
fennel sprigs and bay leaves, to garnish	

MARINADE:

6 teaspoons olive oil	
shredded peel from 1 Seville orange	
6 teaspoons freshly squeezed orange juice	
1 clove garlic, crushed	
6 cardamom pod seeds, removed and crushed	
½ teaspoon salt	
½ teaspoon black pepper	
1 teaspoon Dijon mustard	
2 bay leaves	
3 teaspoons chopped fresh fennel	

Remove scales from the fish and cut off fins and gills using sharp scissors. Rinse under running water and dry on absorbent kitchen paper, then score the flesh on each side.

To make marinade, mix olive oil, orange peel, juice, garlic, cardamom seeds, salt, pepper, mustard, bay leaves and fennel together.

Immerse fish in marinade and turn to coat evenly. Cover with plastic wrap and leave in a cool place for 1 hour.

Preheat a hot grill. Take fish out of marinade and loosely wrap each in a vine leaf. Place on grill and cook for 6 minutes, turning once.

Unwrap each fish and arrange on a serving plate. Add juices from pan to remaining marinade and blend together with arrowroot. Put in a saucepan and bring to the boil, stirring, and cook for 1 minute, until thickened and glossy.

Pour sauce over fish and garnish with fennel and bay leaves.

Serves 4.

4 salmon steaks, about 500 g (1 lb), skinned and boned	
90 g (3 oz/⅓ cup) unsalted butter	
185 g (6 oz) oyster mushrooms, thinly sliced	
4 sheets filo pastry, thawed if frozen	
2 teaspoons arrowroot	
3 teaspoons single (light) cream	
fennel sprigs and pink peppercorns, to garnish	

MARINADE:

2 teaspoons light soft brown sugar	
6 teaspoons rosé wine	
6 teaspoons raspberry vinegar	
2 teaspoons pink peppercorns, crushed	
4 teaspoons chopped fresh fennel	
4 teaspoons chopped fresh oregano	

Mix the marinade ingredients together, pour over the salmon in a shallow dish and turn to coat evenly. Cover with plastic wrap and leave in a cool place for 1 hour.

Preheat oven to 200C (400F/Gas 6). Melt 30 g (1 oz/6 teaspoons) butter in a small saucepan, add mushrooms, reserving a few for garnish, and fry quickly. Drain, reserving the liquid, then cool.

Melt remaining butter. Brush each sheet of filo pastry with melted butter and fold in half. Take 1 salmon steak at a time, drain well and place in centre of 1 folded piece of pastry. Top with one quarter mushroom slices and wrap up neatly. Place on a buttered baking sheet; repeat to make 4 parcels. Brush with remaining butter.

Cook for 15 minutes, until pastry is crisp and lightly browned. Mix marinade, mushroom liquid and arrowroot in a pan. Bring to boil and cook 1 minute; stir in cream.

Garnish salmon and serve with cream sauce.

Serves 4.

STUFFED QUAIL IN PORT

DUCK WITH KUMQUATS

4 oven-ready quails
fresh herb sprigs, to garnish

MARINADE:

90 ml (3 fl oz/⅓ cup) ruby port
6 teaspoons olive oil
3 teaspoons chopped fresh thyme
3 teaspoons chopped fresh oregano
3 teaspoons chopped fresh winter savory
1 clove garlic, crushed
½ teaspoon each salt and pepper

STUFFING:

30 g (1 oz) shallots
185 g (6 oz) button mushrooms
3 teaspoons chopped fresh parsley
125 g (4 oz) smoked streaky bacon, rinded and chopped

Cut feet and wing tips off each quail. Using kitchen scissors, split quails lengthwise, cutting through one side of backbone from neck to tail. Lay quails flat on a board with breast side uppermost and press to flatten, breaking backbone.

Make a slit between legs through flap of skin, then insert legs and pull through to secure. Loosen skin at breast end of bird for stuffing.

Mix marinade ingredients together, add quails and turn to coat. Cover and leave in a cool place 4 hours. To make stuffing, finely chop shallots, mushrooms and parsley. Add ½ teaspoon salt and pepper.

Heat a frying pan, and fry bacon until fat runs. Add mushroom mixture and fry until dry. Cool. Meanwhile, preheat grill.

Remove quail from marinade and insert stuffing under skin. Arrange on grill rack; brush with marinade. Cook for 10 minutes, turning once and basting with more marinade if necessary.

Arrange on a warmed serving dish and garnish with herbs.

Serves 4.

90 g (3 oz) young spinach leaves, trimmed
4 duck breast fillets, skinned
155 ml (5 fl oz/⅔ cup) dry white wine
pinch ground ginger
8 coriander seeds, crushed
salt and pepper
12 kumquats, sliced
3 tablespoons hazelnut oil
2 teaspoons lemon juice
pomegranate seeds, to garnish

Wash and dry spinach and arrange on 4 plates.

Put duck breasts into a frying pan and pour over the wine. Add ginger and coriander. Season with salt and pepper. Cover pan and simmer for 10 minutes until duck is tender. Add kumquats and simmer for 1 minute. Remove duck and kumquats from pan with a slotted spoon and set aside.

Simmer the liquid in the pan until reduced to 60 ml (2 fl oz/¼ cup). Stir in oil and lemon juice and warm through.

Slice the duck and arrange on the plates with the kumquats. Pour over dressing, then serve garnished with pomegranate seeds.

Serves 4.

PHEASANT IN MADEIRA

ROAST DUCK IN FRUIT SAUCE

1 oven-ready pheasant
30 g (1 oz/6 teaspoons) butter
4 teaspoons plain flour
6 teaspoons single (light) cream

MARINADE:
1 teaspoon clear honey
2 teaspoons finely grated grapefruit peel
6 teaspoons chopped fresh purple basil
6 teaspoons snipped fresh chives
1 teaspoon dry mustard
½ teaspoon salt
½ teaspoon black pepper
155 ml (5 fl oz/⅔ cup) Madeira
6 teaspoons olive oil
4 figs, cut into quarters
125 g (4 oz/1 cup) cherries, stoned

GARNISH:
1 fresh fig, sliced
8 cherries
grapefruit segments
watercress sprigs

Cut pheasant into 4 joints, trim off excess skin; remove wing bones.

To make marinade, mix honey, grapefruit peel, basil, chives, mustard, salt, pepper, Madeira and oil together, then add fruit.

Add joints to marinade turning to coat. Cover with plastic wrap and leave in a cool place for 4 hours.

Preheat oven to 180C (350F/Gas 4). Melt butter in a frying pan, take joints out of marinade and fry quickly to brown. Add marinade, bring to the boil and pour into casserole dish. Cook for 1 hour or until pheasant is tender and juices run clear when pricked with knife.

Arrange pheasant joints on a warmed serving dish and keep warm. Skim fat off marinade. Blend flour and cream, add to marinade and bring to boil, stirring, until thick. Cook gently for 2 minutes, pour over pheasant, then garnish.

Serves 4.

2.25 kg (4½ lb) duck
3 onions, chopped
125 g (4 oz/1 cup) chopped mixed nuts
60 g (2 oz/1 cup) fresh breadcrumbs
4 tablespoons chopped fresh coriander
salt and cayenne pepper
1 egg yolk
3 teaspoons Garam Masala, see page 13
2 tablespoons vegetable oil
2 garlic cloves, crushed
2.5 cm (1 in) piece fresh root ginger, grated
1 teaspoon turmeric
6 teaspoons ground coriander
1 teaspoon chick-pea flour
315 ml (10 fl oz/1¼ cups) natural yogurt
juice of 2 lemons and 2 oranges

Preheat oven to 190C (375F/Gas 5). Wash duck and pat dry with absorbent kitchen paper, then prick skin with a fork.

In a bowl, mix 1 onion, nuts, breadcrumbs, 3 tablespoons fresh coriander, salt and cayenne pepper and yolk together. Use to stuff duck, then truss neatly.

Rub garam masala into skin, place duck in a roasting tin and cook for 1¼ hours or until tender. Remove duck and keep warm.

Heat oil in a saucepan, add remaining onions and cook, stirring, for 5 minutes, until soft. Stir in garlic, ginger, turmeric, ground coriander, salt and cayenne pepper to taste and flour. Cook for 1 minute, then stir in yogurt. Simmer for 10 minutes, then stir in lemon and orange juices and heat gently, without boiling.

Carve duck, pour over sauce and sprinkle with remaining coriander. Serve hot.

Serves 4.

Note: This looks very attractrive garnished with spirals of lemon and orange peel.

GINGER PORK & LYCHEES

2 tablespoons light sesame oil
500 g (1 lb) pork fillet, cut into strips
1 clove garlic, crushed
1 tablespoon chopped fresh ginger
90 g (3 oz) mange tout (snow peas), cut into thin strips
470 g (15 oz) can lychees, drained
½ head Chinese leaves
chilli flowers, to garnish

SWEET AND SOUR DRESSING:

2 tablespoons light sesame oil
4 teaspoons rice vinegar
2 teaspoons dark soy sauce
1 teaspoon honey
1 teaspoon tomato purée (paste)

Heat oil in a large frying pan or wok, add pork, garlic and ginger and cook until pork is lightly browned. Add mange tout (snow peas) and cook for 30 seconds. Remove from heat, transfer with a slotted spoon, and add lychees.

To make the dressing, mix ingredients together in a bowl. Pour over salad, then leave to cool.

Shred Chinese leaves, arrange on serving platter or dishes. Spoon salad on top, garnish and serve.

Serves 4.

SPICED HONEY GAMMON

1.5 kg (3 lb) joint wood-smoked gammon
finely shredded peel and juice of 2 oranges
6 teaspoons clear honey
1 teaspoon ground mace
1 teaspoon grated fresh root ginger
125 g (4 oz) kumquats, sliced
6 teaspoons whole cloves
3 teaspoons cornflour

Soak gammon joint overnight in a bowl of cold water. Drain, transfer to a large saucepan and cover with fresh cold water. Bring to boil, cover and cook for 30 minutes. Drain and cool. Remove skin from gammon, leaving a layer of fat on surface of gammon.

Score fat on the surface of gammon into a lattice pattern with a sharp knife. Preheat oven to 190C (375F/Gas 5); place gammon in roasting tin. In a bowl, mix together orange peel, juice, honey, mace and ginger until evenly blended. Brush a little mixture over surface of gammon and bake in the oven for 30 minutes. Remove gammon from oven, brush surface with more orange mixture. Cover surface of gammon with kumquat slices, held in position with whole cloves.

Return to oven for a further 30-40 minutes until gammon is golden brown and tender. Remove and place on a serving dish. Keep warm. Add 185 ml (6 fl oz/¾ cup) water to roasting tin, stir to mix juices, then strain into a saucepan. Blend cornflour with remaining orange juice and honey mixture, add to pan, bring to boil and cook for 1 minute. Pour into a jug and serve with gammon. Garnish with remaining kumquat slices.

Serves 8.

POMEGRANATE & LIME LAMB

JUNIPER LAMB

4 double lamb chops, about 625 g (1¼ lb)
red currant strands and thyme sprigs, to garnish

MARINADE:
2 pomegranates, peeled
finely grated peel of 1 lime
3 teaspoons freshly squeezed lime juice
3 teaspoons red currant jelly
3 teaspoons chopped fresh thyme
¼ teaspoon salt
½ teaspoon black pepper

SAUCE:
30 g (1 oz/6 teaspoons) butter
1 small red onion, thinly sliced
15 g (½ oz/6 teaspoons) plain flour

To make marinade, scrape pomegranate seeds into a sieve over a bowl, reserving a few for garnish. Press remainder through sieve with a wooden spoon to extract juice.

Put 4 teaspoons juice in another bowl with marinade ingredients.

Put chops in a shallow dish and brush each with marinade to coat evenly. Cover with plastic wrap and leave for 1 hour in a cool place.

Preheat a moderately hot grill. Grill chops for 5-8 minutes on each side, turning once and brushing with marinade. Keep warm.

Melt butter in saucepan, add onion and cook gently for 1-2 minutes, until tender. Stir in flour and cook for 1 minute, stirring, then remove saucepan from heat. Make up remaining pomegranate juice to 250 ml (8 fl oz/1 cup) with juices from the grill pan and water. Stir into saucepan, bring to the boil, stirring, and cook 2 minutes.

Pour a little sauce onto a warmed serving plate, arrange chops on top and garnish with currant strands, reserved seeds and thyme sprigs.

Serves 4.

625 g (1¼ lb) loin of lamb, well trimmed and boned
4 teaspoons plain flour

MARINADE:
250 ml (8 fl oz/1 cup) rosé wine
4 teaspoons juniper berries, crushed
2 teaspoons Angostura bitters
2 bay leaves
½ teaspoon salt
½ teaspoon black pepper

STUFFING:
60 g (2 oz/1 cup) fresh white breadcrumbs
60 g (2 oz) pre-soaked dried apricots
2 teaspoons lemon juice
2 teaspoons finely grated lemon peel
2 teaspoons chopped fresh rosemary

GARNISH:
lemon wedges
6 apricots
rosemary sprigs

To make marinade, mix all ingredients together, add lamb and turn to coat evenly. Cover and leave in a cool place for 4 hours or overnight.

Preheat oven to 190C (375F/Gas 5). To make stuffing, process bread, apricots, lemon juice, peel and rosemary in a food processor.

Remove lamb from marinade and pat dry. Spread stuffing over centre of meat, roll up, and tie securely in several places. Place in roasting tin, brush well with marinade and cook for 45-50 minutes, basting with marinade if necessary. Place meat on a serving plate; keep warm.

Stir flour into tin, add remaining marinade and bring to the boil, stirring; add a little water if too thick. Strain into serving bowl.

Remove string from meat, cut meat into thin slices and pour some sauce over a serving plate. Arrange lamb in centre and garnish.

Serves 4-6.

CHICKEN IN GINGER SAUCE

CRISPY GRAPEFRUIT CHICKEN

four 185 g (6 oz) boneless chicken breasts (fillets), skinned
2 tablespoons vegetable oil
6 spring onions, finely chopped
3 cloves garlic, crushed
5 cm (2 in) piece fresh root ginger, grated
1 teaspoon ground cumin
2 teaspoons Garam Masala, see page 13
salt and pepper
3 teaspoons lemon juice
6 tablespoons hot water
parsley sprigs and lemon slices, to garnish

Wash chicken, pat dry with absorbent kitchen paper and slice thinly.

Heat oil in a large frying pan, add onions and fry for 2-3 minutes, stirring, to soften. Remove from pan with a slotted spoon. Put chicken in pan and fry over a high heat, stirring frequently, for about 5 minutes or until browned all over.

Stir in garlic, ginger, cumin and garam masala and season with salt and pepper. Cook for 1 minute, then stir in onions, lemon juice and water. Cover and cook over a low heat for about 10 minutes or until chicken is tender. Serve hot, garnished with parsley and lemon.

Serves 4.

8 chicken thighs, about 1.25 kg (2 lb)
grapefruit segments and rosemary sprigs, to garnish

MARINADE:
3 teaspoons chopped fresh rosemary
3 teaspoons clear honey
60 ml (2 fl oz/¼ cup) olive oil
¾ teaspoon cayenne pepper
2 teaspoons finely grated grapefruit peel
6 teaspoons freshly squeezed grapefruit juice

To make marinade, mix rosemary, honey, olive oil, cayenne, grapefruit peel and juice together until well blended.

Place chicken thighs in a shallow ovenproof dish, pour over marinade and turn chicken until evenly coated. Cover with plastic wrap and leave to marinate in a cool place for 3-4 hours.

Preheat oven to 220C (425F/Gas 7). Cook chicken for 20-25 minutes, until golden brown and skin is crisp, basting with marinade periodically, if necessary.

Arrange chicken on a serving plate and garnish with grapefruit segments and rosemary sprigs.

Serves 4.

HORSERADISH STEAK

STEAK AU POIVRE

500 g (1 lb) rump steak, cut into
thin strips

30 g (1 oz/6 teaspoons) butter

6 teaspoons sherry

thyme sprigs, to garnish

MARINADE:

4 teaspoons horseradish sauce

4 teaspoons strained Greek yogurt

2 teaspoons paprika

3 teaspoons chopped fresh thyme

½ teaspoon salt

½ teaspoon black pepper

To make marinade, mix horseradish,
yogurt, paprika, thyme, salt and
pepper together, stirring until well

blended. Add meat and stir to coat
evenly. Cover with plastic wrap and
leave in a cool place for 1 hour.

Melt butter in frying pan.
Remove steak from marinade using
a slotted spoon, add to frying pan
and cook quickly for 1 minute. Lift
strips of steak out and place on a
serving dish.

Stir remaining marinade and
sherry into pan and bring to the
boil, stirring well. Pour over steak
on serving dish and garnish with a
few sprigs of fresh thyme.

Serves 4.

1½ teaspoons green peppercorns

1 teaspoon black peppercorns

1 teaspoon white peppercorns

4 rump steaks, each weighing about
185 g (6 oz)

45 g (1½ oz/9 teaspoons) unsalted butter

few drops Tabasco sauce

few drops Worcestershire sauce

2 tablespoons brandy

3 tablespoons double (thick) cream

salt

sauté or jacket baked potatoes and green
salad, to serve

Coarsely crush all peppercorns in a
pestle and mortar.

Sprinkle crushed pepper over
both sides of steaks, pressing in well
with palm of hand. Set aside for 30
minutes. Melt 15 g (½ oz/3 teaspoons) butter in a large frying pan
and heat until foaming. Add steaks
and cook for 2-3 minutes, then turn

and cook other sides for 2-3
minutes. (This timing gives
medium-rare steaks, so adjust
cooking time to suit personal
preference). Turn steaks once again
and top each one with 7 g (¼ oz/
1½ teaspoons) butter and sprinkle
with a few drops Tabasco sauce and
Worcestershire sauce.

Pour over brandy and allow to
heat through for a few seconds. Set
it alight and remove from heat.
When flames subside, lift steaks
from pan and arrange on a warmed
serving plate and keep warm. Add
cream to pan, stir well and heat
through for 1 minute, scraping up
sediment from pan. Season with
salt and spoon mixture over steaks.
Serve at once with sauté or jacket
baked potatoes and a green salad.

Serves 4.

ROSTI

750 g (1½ lb) potatoes, scrubbed
1 small onion
4 rashers smoked streaky bacon
60 g (2 oz) Austrian smoked cheese
salt and pepper
45 g (1½ oz/9 teaspoons) butter
basil sprigs, to garnish

Put potatoes into a saucepan of salted water, bring to the boil and simmer for 5 minutes. Remove from the heat, drain and allow to get cold.

Coarsely grate potatoes and onion into a large bowl. Remove the rind from the bacon and cut the bacon into very thin strips. Cut cheese into small chunks and, using 2 forks, toss the bacon and cheese into the potato mixture and season with salt and pepper.

Melt butter in a large frying pan, add the grated mixture and cook over a moderate heat for 10-15 minutes. Then press well together, turn over and cook the other side for a further 5 minutes. Turn out onto a warmed plate, cut into wedges and serve at once, garnished with sprigs of basil.

Serves 4.

FRAGRANT FRIED RICE

185 g (6 oz/1¼ cups) basmati rice
3 tablespoons vegetable oil
8 cloves
4 black cardamom pods, bruised
1 bay leaf
7.5 cm (3 in) cinnamon stick
1 teaspoon black peppercorns
1 teaspoon cumin seeds
1 teaspoon coriander seeds
1 onion, sliced into rings
1 small cauliflower, cut into tiny flowerets
salt
onion rings and bay leaves, to garnish

Place rice in a sieve and wash under cold running water until water runs clear. Put in a bowl with 625 ml (20 fl oz/2½ cups) water and soak for 30 minutes. Heat oil in a heavy-based saucepan, add cloves, cardamom pods, bay leaf, cinnamon, peppercorns and cumin and coriander seeds and fry for 1 minute. Add onion and cook for 5 minutes, until softened. Drain rice and reserve the soaking water.

Add rice to the pan and fry for 2-3 minutes, until opaque and light golden. Stir in reserved water and cauliflower and season with salt. Bring to the boil, lower heat and simmer, covered, for 12-15 minutes, stirring once or twice, until liquid is absorbed and rice and cauliflower are tender. Serve hot, garnished with onion rings and bay leaves.

Serves 4.

Note: Do not eat the whole spices.

POLANAISE CRUMBLE

CREAMED SPINACH & CELERY

250 g (8 oz) cauliflower flowerets	
250 g (8 oz) broccoli flowerets	

TOPPING:

30 g (1 oz/6 teaspoons) butter	
60 g (2 oz/1 cup) soft white breadcrumbs	
3 teaspoons chopped fresh parsley	
1 hard-boiled egg, sieved	

SAUCE:

30 g (1 oz/6 teaspoons) butter	
30 g (1 oz/¼ cup) plain flour	
315 ml (10 fl oz/1¼ cups) milk	
salt and ground black pepper	

To make topping, heat butter in a pan, add breadcrumbs and fry until golden. Put in a bowl; add parsley and egg.

To make sauce, put butter, flour, milk and salt and pepper to taste in a saucepan. Whisk together over a moderate heat until thick. Cook for 1-2 minutes, then keep warm.

Cook cauliflower and broccoli in boiling, salted water for 3-4 minutes until just tender. Drain and place in a warmed serving dish. Pour over sauce and sprinkle over topping. Serve hot.

Serves 4-6.

1 kg (2 lb) spinach	
6 sticks celery	
30 g (1 oz/6 teaspoons) butter	
1 teaspoon grated nutmeg	
90 ml (3 fl oz/⅓ cup) double (thick) cream	
¼ teaspoon salt	
½ teaspoon ground black pepper	

Stem and wash spinach; wash and thinly slice celery. Cook celery and spinach separately in boiling, salted water until just tender. Drain each vegetable thoroughly, pressing out excess water from spinach.

Line bases and sides of 8 warmed individual soufflé dishes with a few whole spinach leaves. Chop remaining spinach roughly. Melt butter in a saucepan, add nutmeg, cream and salt and pepper and bring to the boil. Add spinach and toss well.

Half-fill each soufflé dish with spinach mixture, cover each with a layer of celery, reserving a little for garnish, and fill each up to the top with remaining spinach. Press firmly. Just before serving, invert spinach moulds onto a serving plate and garnish with reserved celery slices. Serve warm.

Serves 8.

SPICY OKRA

375 g (12 oz) okra
2 tablespoons vegetable oil
2.5 cm (1 in) piece fresh root ginger, grated
1 teaspoon turmeric
½ teaspoon chilli powder
1 teaspoon chick-pea flour
salt
315 ml (10 fl oz/1¼ cups) natural yogurt
2 tablespoons chopped fresh coriander, to garnish

Wash okra and pat dry with absorbent kitchen paper, then cut into thick slices.

Heat oil in a saucepan, add okra and fry, stirring occasionally, for 4 minutes. Stir in ginger, turmeric, chilli powder and flour. Season with salt and fry for 1 minute more.

Stir in 3 tablespoons water, then cover and cook gently for 10 minutes or until okra is tender. Stir in yogurt and reheat gently. Serve hot, sprinkled with coriander.

Serves 4.

Note: Choose okra pods that are about 10 cm (4 in) long – larger pods are tough and stringy to eat.

JAPANESE VINEGARED SALAD

125 g (4 oz) mange tout (snow peas), trimmed
185 g (6 oz/1 cup) long grain rice

JAPANESE DRESSING:
2 tablespoons rice vinegar
1 tablespoon light sesame oil
1 teaspoon dark sesame oil
4 teaspoons tamari (Japanese soy sauce)
4 spring onions, chopped

Blanch the mange tout (snow peas) in a saucepan of boiling water for 30 seconds, drain, rinse under cold water, then dry on absorbent kitchen paper. Arrange around edge of serving dish.

Cook rice in boiling salted water for 10-12 minutes until tender. Drain, rinse with cold water, then drain again. Put rice into a bowl. To make the dressing, mix ingredients together in a bowl or screw-top jar. Stir into rice. Spoon rice into serving dish and serve.

Serves 4-6.

Variation: The dressed rice can be wrapped in small blanched spinach or vine leaves. Cut the parcels in half, then stand them on end to resemble Japanese sushi.

COURGETTE SALAD

CUCUMBER & DILL SALAD

500 g (1 lb) courgettes (zucchini), coarsely grated
salt
fresh herbs or baby courgettes (zucchini) and flowers, to garnish

HERB YOGURT MAYONNAISE:
2 tablespoons mayonnaise
2 teaspoons chopped fresh parsley
2 teaspoons chopped fresh tarragon
2 teaspoons chopped fresh chervil
2 teaspoons chopped fresh chives
60 ml (2 fl oz/¼ cup) natural yogurt
pepper

Place courgettes (zucchini) on 3 layers of absorbent kitchen paper, sprinkle with salt and leave for 1 hour.

To make the dressing, mix all the ingredients together in a large bowl. Add courgettes (zucchini) to dressing and stir together. Spoon into a serving dish and serve garnished with fresh herbs or baby courgettes (zucchini) and flowers.

Serves 6.

1 large cucumber
salt
4 teaspoons lemon juice or white wine vinegar
black pepper, if desired
1 tablespoon chopped fresh dill

Peel cucumber, reserving a few strips of peel. Cut cucumber in half lengthwise and hollow out the seeds with a teaspoon. Slice thinly, then put into a colander, sprinkle with salt and leave to drain for 30 minutes. Rinse with cold water and dry on absorbent paper.

Put cucumber into a bowl and sprinkle with lemon juice or vinegar. Season with pepper, if desired, then stir in dill and serve garnished with strips of cucumber peel.

Serves 4-6.

PEACH CREAM BRÛLÉE

2 egg yolks
3 teaspoons caster sugar
few drops vanilla essence
315 ml (10 fl oz/1¼ cups) double (thick) cream
3 ripe peaches
250 g (8 oz/1¼ cups) demerara sugar

Beat together egg yolks, caster sugar and vanilla essence until pale and fluffy. Heat cream until just boiling and whisk onto the egg mixture.

Return to the pan and cook over a low heat, stirring continuously until thickened. Do not allow to boil. Remove from the heat and allow to cool slightly.

Peel, halve and stone peaches and place half a peach in the bottom of 6 ramekin dishes. Pour the cooled custard over the peaches and refrigerate for 6-12 hours until firm.

Sprinkle over a thick layer of demerara sugar and place under a very hot grill until sugar dissolves and bubbles. Allow the topping to cool before serving.

Serves 6.

COEURS À LA CRÈME

250 g (8 oz) ricotta or cottage cheese
30 g (1 oz/5 teaspoons) caster sugar
1 teaspoon lemon juice
315 ml (10 fl oz/1¼ cups) double (thick) cream
2 egg whites

TO SERVE:
fresh fruit and double (thick) cream

Line 8 heart-shaped moulds with muslin. Press cheese through a sieve into a bowl. Stir in sugar and lemon juice.

In a separate bowl, whip cream until stiff. Stir into cheese mixture.

Whisk egg whites until stiff, then fold into the cheese mixture.

Spoon into moulds, place on 2 plates and leave to drain overnight in the refrigerator.

To serve, unmould onto individual plates and gently remove the muslin. Serve the hearts with fresh fruit with cream handed separately.

Serves 8.

Note: To add extra colour, decorate with sprigs of red and black currants.

ROSE CREAM

625 ml (20 fl oz/2½ cups) whipping cream
3 teaspoons powdered gelatine
5-6 teaspoons triple strength rosewater
grated peel and juice of 1 lemon
60 g (2 oz/¼ cup) caster sugar

ROSE PETALS:

1 egg white
petals from 1 rose
caster sugar

To prepare rose petals, preheat oven to 110C (225F/Gas ¼). Whisk egg white until frothy and dip rose petals in to cover.

Toss petals in caster sugar and place on baking tray covered with silicone paper. Bake in the bottom of oven for about 2½ hours, leaving oven door slightly ajar, until dry and hard. Place all ingredients for cream in a heavy-based saucepan and stir over a very low heat until gelatine and sugar have dissolved. Do not allow to boil.

Pour into 6 ramekin dishes and cool at room temperature. Chill creams in refrigerator until ready to serve, then decorate with the frosted rose petals.

Serves 6.

Note: The rose petals can be prepared in advance and stored in an airtight tin. For extra colour, decorate with frosted rose leaves as well as petals but do not eat them.

HOT CHOCOLATE SOUFFLÉ

2 tablespoons caster sugar
125 g (4 oz) plain (dark) chocolate
2 tablespoons brandy or coffee
4 eggs, separated, plus 2 extra whites
icing sugar, to serve

Preheat oven to 200C (400F/Gas 6). Butter a 1 litre (32 fl oz/4 cup) soufflé dish and dust out with 1 tablespoon caster sugar. Break chocolate into pieces and put into a double boiler or a bowl set over a saucepan of simmering water with the brandy or coffee.

Set over medium heat and stir until smooth. Take care not to overheat the chocolate or it will lose its gloss and become very thick and difficult to combine with other ingredients. Remove from heat and beat in egg yolks with remaining caster sugar. In a bowl, whisk egg whites until stiff but not dry. Fold 1 tablespoon into chocolate mixture, then scrape into egg whites and quickly fold together using a metal spoon.

Pour into prepared soufflé dish, place on a baking sheet and bake in the oven for 15-18 minutes, until risen and just set. Serve immediately, dusted with icing sugar.

Serves 4.

PINEAPPLE ALASKA

FIG & PORT ICE CREAM

1 large ripe pineapple with leaves
1-2 tablespoons kirsch
1 litre (32 fl oz/4 cups) vanilla ice cream
3 egg whites
185 g (6 oz/¾ cup) caster sugar
1 tablespoon caster sugar for sprinkling

Cut pineapple and leafy 'plume' in half lengthwise. Using a grapefruit knife, cut out flesh. Discard core, then cut flesh into chunks and put into a bowl. Sprinkle with kirsch, cover with plastic wrap and chill overnight with pineapple shells.

Put pineapple chunks back into shells and pack ice cream on top. Put in freezer for about 2 hours, until very firm. Meanwhile, pre-heat oven to 200C (400F/Gas 6). Just before serving, whisk egg whites in a bowl until stiff. Whisk in half the sugar, whisking for 1 minute more. Then fold in remaining sugar.

Pile this meringue over ice cream, making sure it is completely covered. Make small peaks in meringue with a flat-bladed knife. Place pineapple shells on a baking sheet and sprinkle with the 1 table-spoon caster sugar. Bake in the oven for about 8 minutes, until meringue is browned. Serve immediately.

Serves 6.

Variation: Try making this dessert using a fruit sorbet instead of ice cream.

125 g (4 oz/½ cup) caster sugar
155 ml (5 fl oz/⅔ cup) ruby port
4 cm (1½ in) cinnamon stick
6 fresh figs
4 teaspoons freshly squeezed lime juice
315 ml (10 fl oz/1¼ cups) double (thick) cream
fresh fig slices and mint leaves, to decorate

Place sugar and port in a saucepan and heat gently, stirring occasion-ally, until sugar has melted. Bring to the boil, then add cinnamon stick and figs, cover and cook very gently for 5 minutes. Leave the figs in the marinade, still covered, until they are completely cold.

Transfer figs and liquor to a food processor fitted with a metal blade and process until smooth.

Pour mixture into a sieve over a bowl and rub through using a wooden spoon. Stir in lime juice.

Whip cream until thick, then fold into fig purée until evenly blended. Pour mixture into a plastic container, cover and freeze for 1-2 hours, until almost frozen.

Return mixture to food processor and process until thick and smooth. Return to plastic container and freeze until firm. Scoop ice cream to serve, then decorate.

Serves 4.

KUMQUAT CRANBERRY TARTS

INDIVIDUAL PEAR PUFFS

WALNUT PASTRY:
185 g (6 oz/1½ cups) plain flour
125 g (4 oz/½ cup) butter
60 g (2 oz/½ cup) chopped walnuts
60 g (2 oz/¼ cup) caster sugar
1 egg, beaten

FILLING:
185 g (6 oz/¾ cup) caster sugar
250 g (8 oz) kumquats, sliced
250 g (8 oz/1½ cups) cranberries
185 g (6 oz/¾ cup) cream cheese
90 ml (3 fl oz/⅓ cup) Greek yogurt
1 teaspoon arrowroot

To make pastry, sift the flour into a bowl.

Add butter and rub in to form breadcrumbs. Stir in walnuts, sugar and enough egg to form a soft dough. Knead and roll out the pastry to line six 12 cm (4½ in) fluted flan tins.

Trim edges and prick bases; chill 30 minutes.

Preheat oven to 190C (375F/Gas 5). Heat sugar and 250 ml (8 fl oz/1 cup) water until dissolved. Bring to boil, add kumquats; cook for 3 minutes. Strain; return ⅓ syrup to pan; reserve remaining syrup. Add cranberries to syrup in pan, bring to boil, cover and cook for 3 minutes.

Strain, keeping individual syrups and fruit separate. Bake tart cases in oven for 10-15 minutes until lightly browned. Cool. Beat cream cheese with yogurt. Spread over base of tarts. Arrange alternate circles of fruit in tarts. Blend ½ teaspoon arrowroot into each syrup; bring each to boil. Glaze kumquats with clear syrup and cranberries with red syrup. Leave to set.

Serves 6.

250 g (8 oz) puff pastry, thawed if frozen
2 large, ripe eating pears
1 egg yolk
1 tablespoon milk
caster sugar for sprinkling
Poire William liqueur, if desired

Preheat oven to 220C (425F/Gas 7). Roll out pastry to a rough rectangle, about 0.5 cm (¼ in) thick. Using a pear (halved, if easier) as a guide, cut out a pastry pear shape, 1 cm (½ in) larger than the pear.

Cut directly round pear, leaving a pear-shaped 'frame'. Roll out solid pear shape to same size as frame, dampen edges with water and fit frame on top. Press edges together lightly, then 'knock up' using a blunt knife. Make 3 more pastry pear shapes in same way.

Peel and halve pears. Scoop out cores with a teaspoon, then cut across into thin slices. Fit neatly into pastry shapes.

Place pear puffs on baking sheet. Beat egg yolk with milk in a small bowl and brush edges of pastry with this. Bake in the oven for 15-20 minutes, until pears are tender and pastry edges are puffed up and golden. Remove from oven, sprinkle with caster sugar and place under a hot grill for 1 minute. Transfer to serving plates. Heat liqueur, if using, in a small saucepan, set alight and pour, flaming, over puffs. Serve at once.

Serves 4.

CHILDREN'S PARTIES

Children's parties usually centre around a birthday celebration. As such, it is one of the most important times of the year for the child. To help make the occasion enjoyable and fun for everyone, the recipes on the following pages are easy to make and easy to eat. Along with sweet drinks and a birthday cake are some unique dishes that transform standard, healthy food into colourful fun food, which is appealing to any child. Many of these dishes can also be made in part by the children themselves. This will keep them occupied while you are organising the next event. Children are also more likely to eat food that they have helped make themselves.

PLANNING PARTIES

When planning a children's party, try to keep the age groups more or less the same. Five to eight year-olds will play well together as do nine to twelve year-olds. The duration of the party for children of this age should be about 2 to 2½ hours. You may wish to make the party longer, however, it is usually beneficial to all concerned to keep the party short but highly active. Very small children (under-fives) are harder to organise and may not have the skill for some of the games. It is best to limit the duration of their party to 1½ hours.

Draw up a list of the guests with your child, but do consider the amount of room you have available and that just a few children can seem like very many. If your party is held during the summer, make use of a garden, if one is available. It will certainly stand more wear and tear than indoors.

Left: Make these little parcels of sweets from a circle of net (use a dinner plate as a guide). Put sweets, such as sugared almonds, inside. Secure with an elastic band and cover with a ribbon bow. Put one by each table setting.

Right: Teddy bears are great favourites with both children and adults. They are used effectively on this birthday cake and these gingerbread biscuits (see page 78 for recipes).

Send out colourful invitations about two weeks in advance, clearly giving the time, day, date and location of the party. Your child may like to decorate the invitations him or herself.

GAMES & ENTERTAINMENT

Every moment must be organised with children's parties. You may find it advantageous to hire a puppet show, magician or a clown to keep the children quietly entertained.

If you are organising all the activities yourself, alternate boisterous games like 'musical bumps' with quieter ones like 'pinning the tail on the donkey'. Have a cassette player or record player available. It is useful for singing 'Happy Birthday' and for games such as 'musical chairs'.

If you are awarding prizes for winning the games, make sure every child ends up with some sort of small gift. If the game involves teams, it is best that you or another adult picks the teams randomly. A good idea is to give out 'goody' bags – containing a small toy or storybook and balloon – for the children to take home after the party. Vary the bag depending on the age group. Older children may prefer a chocolate bar, a novelty pen and notebook or a miniature deck of cards.

FUN FARE

In this chapter you will find a number of unusual ideas for feeding children of all ages. You may also want to include some of the more traditional children's food, such as small sausages, jelly, milkshakes, and, of course, ice cream and cake.

The size of portions you should serve depends on the age of the children attending the party. Children over eight years old generally have much bigger appetites than smaller children, so adapt your meal plan accordingly. Filling, American-style food is often the perfect answer to hungry stomachs.

For young children, try planning a range of small snacks and finger sandwiches. Peanut-Banana Malties (page 77) and Traffic Lights (page 76) are novel variations on the everyday sandwich. Other recipes suitable for young children include Cowboys' Buns (see page 75) and Pizza or Pancake Faces (see pages 73 and 77). Older children may appreciate more sophisticated dishes such as Cheesy Ham Croissants (page 76) and Chilli Dogs (page 74), or, as savoury titbits, Party Quiches (page 73). All these recipes are both inexpensive and easy to make.

As no birthday party would be complete without a cake, we have also provided the recipe for a 'Teddy Bear' birthday cake (see page 78) that will fascinate and delight both children and adults.

Use these recipes as a guide to creating your own variations. There is no reason why a children's party can't be just as fun for the adult!

PASTRY:

60 g (2 oz/½ cup) plain flour
¼ teaspoon salt
30 g (1 oz/6 teaspoons) butter

FILLING:

1 egg
6 teaspoons single (light) cream
¼ teaspoon salt
¼ teaspoon pepper
¼ teaspoon dry mustard
2 teaspoons each finely chopped peppers (capsicums), chopped button mushrooms, crisp crumbled bacon and fresh herbs

Sift flour and salt into a bowl. Cut the butter into small pieces.

Add butter to bowl and rub in finely until mixture resembles breadcrumbs. Using a fork, stir in 2-3 teaspoons water until mixture begins to bind together. Knead to form a firm dough. Roll out pastry thinly on a lightly floured surface and use to line 24 tiny pastry boat moulds or tiny round tartlet tins. Prick bases and chill for 1 hour. Preheat oven to 220C (425F/Gas 7). Bake pastry moulds for 5 minutes, then remove from oven.

To make filling, put egg, cream, salt, pepper and mustard in a bowl. Whisk until well blended. Half-fill each pastry case with egg mixture, then fill 6 with chopped peppers (capsicums), 6 with mushrooms, 6 with bacon and the remainder with herbs. Return to the oven for a further 5-6 minutes until filling has set. Cool slightly, then slip pastry cases out of moulds. Serve warm or cold.

Makes 24.

freshly-baked or bought, ready-made individual pizza bases

TOPPING:

4 tablespoons tomato ketchup (sauce) or chutney
6-8 processed Cheddar cheese slices
alfalfa sprouts or grated carrot
olive slices
pepper (capsicum) strips

Preheat oven to 200C (400F/Gas 6). Spread pizza bases with ketchup or chutney. Arrange cheese over top to represent skin. Place on a baking sheet and bake in the oven for 10-15 minutes until melted.

Give each child the prepared ingredients to make their own pizza face, using alfalfa sprouts or carrot as hair, olive slices for eyes and pepper (capsicum) strips for mouth.

Serves 2.

Variations: Many other ingredients can be used in place of those listed and children will enjoy making different expressions on the faces.

CHILLI DOGS

3 tablespoons corn oil
1 onion, thinly sliced
1 clove garlic, crushed
1 teaspoon chilli powder
227 g (8 oz) can tomatoes, drained
1 tablespoon tomato purée (paste)
½ teaspoon dry mustard
1 tablespoon malt vinegar
1 tablespoon Worcestershire sauce
1 tablespoon light soft brown sugar
¼ teaspoon salt
225 g (7.94 oz) can barbecue beans
4 frankfurters
4 seeded hot dog rolls
60 g (2 oz/¼ cup) butter, softened

TO GARNISH:

onion rings
chopped spring onion leaves
cress sprigs

Heat 2 tablespoons oil in a saucepan. Add onion, garlic and chilli powder and fry for 2 minutes. Stir in tomatoes and cut up with a knife. Add the tomato purée (paste), mustard, vinegar, Worcestershire sauce, sugar and salt and simmer for 5 minutes. Stir in beans and cook for a further 5 minutes.

Meanwhile, snip frankfurters alternately on both sides at 1 cm (½ in) intervals. Brush with remaining oil and grill for 3-4 minutes, turning frequently until browned.

Cut the hot dog rolls open, but do not cut right through. Open out and spread with butter. Arrange frankfurters in rolls and place a few onion rings along one side of each one. Spoon chilli sauce over frankfurters. Sprinkle with chopped spring onion leaves and garnish with sprigs of cress.

Makes 4.

GIANT SALAD BURGERS

500 g (1 lb) lean ground beef
salt and pepper
3 tablespoons corn oil
2 seeded baps
2 spring onions
3 tablespoons mayonnaise
2 tablespoons mango chutney
2 chunky slices iceberg lettuce
2 slices large beefsteak tomato
4 red pepper (capsicum) rings, seeded
mild pickled chillies and tomato, to garnish

Season beef with salt and pepper, mix well and form into two 10 cm (4 in) diameter burgers. Heat oil in a frying pan. Add burgers and fry for 5-6 minutes on each side, or until cooked as desired.

Meanwhile, split and lightly toast baps. Cut spring onions in half to make 4 short onions and, using a sharp pointed knife, cut to form feathery green ends.

Mix mayonnaise with chutney. Spread bap bases with half the mayonnaise mixture. Arrange slices of lettuce on top and add a slice of tomato to each one. Top with a beefburger and cover with rings of red pepper (capsicum) and feathery spring onions. Spoon remaining mayonnaise mixture on top.

Place bap lids in position and secure in place with cocktail sticks threaded with pickled chillies and tomato.

Makes 2.

Variations: Omit mayonnaise mixture and top with tomato ketchup (sauce) or relishes instead. Add a slice of processed cheese or thin slices of Gruyère cheese.

COWBOYS' BUNS

| 6 crusty white rolls |
| 60 g (2 oz/¼ cup) butter, melted |
| 250 g (8 oz) Dutch pork smoked sausage |
| 1 small onion, finely chopped |
| 220 g (7 oz) can baked beans |
| watercress sprigs, to garnish |

Preheat the oven to 200C (400F/ Gas 6). Cut tops off rolls and set aside. Hollow out centres of rolls, leaving a thin wall of bread. Brush insides of rolls with 45 g (1½ oz/9 teaspoons) of the butter.

Wrap foil around each roll, leaving the top open. Place on a baking sheet and put in the oven for 10 minutes to heat through.

Meanwhile, simmer the sausage in boiling water for 10 minutes. Fry the onion in the remaining butter until slightly softened and transparent. Cut the sausage into thin slices and stir into the onion. Add the beans and heat through.

Remove the foil from the rolls, then spoon in the sausage mixture. Replace the bread tops and return to the oven for a further 2-3 minutes. Garnish with sprigs of watercress and serve at once.

Serves 6.

HAM & PINEAPPLE MUFFINS

| 2 muffins |
| 30 g (1 oz/6 teaspoons) butter |
| 4 slices cooked ham, each 0.5 cm (¼ in) thick |
| 4 thick slices large beefsteak tomato |
| 4 canned pineapple slices, drained |
| 4 teaspoons piccalilli |
| 125 g (4 oz/1 cup) Jarlsberg cheese, grated |
| 60 g (2 oz/½ cup) red-veined Cheddar cheese, grated |
| coriander sprigs, to garnish |

Split and toast muffins, then spread with butter. Using an 8 cm (3½ in) round cutter, cut out 4 rounds from slices of ham. (Use up leftovers in sandwiches.)

Place ham rounds on muffins and top each with a slice of tomato. Pat pineapple slices dry and place on top of ham. Spoon a little piccalilli into each hole in pineapple.

Mix cheeses together and form into mounds on top of pineapple. Cook under a hot grill for 6-7 minutes or until the cheeses are melted, bubbling and lightly golden. Garnish with sprigs of coriander.

Makes 4.

TRAFFIC LIGHTS

CHEESY HAM CROISSANTS

2 large slices brown bread, crusts removed
2 large slices white bread, crusts removed
60 g (2 oz/¼ cup) butter, softened
2 teaspoons thousand island dressing
2 green lettuce leaves, finely shredded
2 hard-boiled eggs, shelled and sliced
5 slices tomato
salt and pepper
spring onion flowers, to garnish

Spread all slices of bread with butter, then spread brown slices with thousand island dressing.

Cover one-third of the area of brown slices with lettuce, reserving a little.

Remove egg yolks from whites and arrange yolk slices over centre area of bread, reserving a little.

Place 4 tomato slices over remaining area on bread. Season with salt and pepper.

Using a small 2 cm (¾ in) round biscuit cutter, cut out 6 holes from each slice of white bread.

Place bread, with buttered sides down, over filling and press together firmly. Cut each sandwich neatly in half to form 'traffic lights'.

Chop reserved lettuce and tomato and slice egg yolk; use to fill the relevant holes in sandwich.

Garnish with onion flowers.

Makes 4.

Variation: Use slices of cheese in place of hard-boiled egg.

4 thin slices smoked ham
1 teaspoon prepared mild mustard
1 teaspoon chopped fresh chives
4 thin slices Gouda cheese
4 croissants

Preheat the oven to 200C (400F/ Gas 6). Spread ham slices with mustard and sprinkle chives over cheese slices. Cut each slice of ham and each slice of cheese into two.

Place a slice of cheese on top of one slice of ham, top with the second ham slice and finish with cheese. Repeat until you have 4 ham and cheese stacks.

Split croissants in half and put a stack into each. Enclose croissants in foil and bake in the oven for 10 minutes.

Remove from the oven and open up the foil. Return to the oven for a further 2 minutes until the croissants are crisp. Serve at once.

Serves 4.

PEANUT-BANANA MALTIES

FUNNY FACE PANCAKES

3 thin slices malt bread
2 tablespoons crunchy peanut butter
1 banana
1 tablespoon lemon juice
¼-½ teaspoon ground cinnamon
1 teaspoon light soft brown sugar
60 g (2 oz) full fat soft cheese
2 chunky wedges green or red eating apple, to decorate

Spread 1 slice of malt bread with 1 tablespoon peanut butter. Cut off 2 slices from banana, dip in lemon juice and reserve for decoration. Cut remaining banana in half cross-wise and then into thin lengthwise slices. Dip in lemon juice. Mix together cinnamon and sugar.

Cover peanut butter with half quantity of banana slices and sprinkle with cinnamon sugar.

Spread a slice of bread with cheese and place, cheese-side down, over sliced banana. Spread this slice of bread with remaining peanut butter and cover with remaining long slices of banana. Sprinkle with cinnamon sugar.

Spread remaining slice of bread with remaining cheese and place over banana.

Press sandwich firmly together and cut diagonally in half. Secure each one with a cocktail stick. Dip wedges of apple into lemon juice. Thread reserved slices of banana and apple wedges onto cocktail sticks. Sprinkle both halves with remaining cinnamon sugar and serve at once.

Makes 2.

125 g (4 oz/1 cup) plain flour
pinch salt
1 egg
315 ml (10 fl oz/1¼ cups) milk
grated rind of ½ lemon
vegetable oil
3 tablespoons strawberry conserve, sieved
2 teaspoons lemon juice
8 blueberries
4 strawberries
90 g (3 oz/1¾ cups) shredded coconut
60 g (2 oz/½ cup) toasted flaked almonds

Sift together flour and salt into a large bowl. Add egg, milk and lemon rind and beat to form a smooth batter.

Heat a 17.5 cm (7 in) pancake pan and brush with a little oil. Pour in some batter and cook for 1 minute until the underside of the pancake is golden, then turn over and cook the other side for 1 minute.

Remove from the pan and keep warm between 2 plates set over a pan of simmering water. Repeat until all the batter is used up and you have 8 pancakes.

Mix jam and lemon juice together. Cut out eyes, 2 nostrils and a mouth from 4 of the pancakes. Spread remaining pancakes with jam and top with 'face' pancakes. Put a blueberry into each eye, 2 strips of coconut as eyebrows and slices of strawberries for cheeks.

Mix together the rest of the coconut and the almonds and arrange round the edge of the pancake face as hair. Serve at once.

Serves 4.

GINGERBEAR BISCUITS

125 g (8 oz/2 cups) plain flour
25 g (3 oz/⅓ cup) margarine or butter
25 g (3 oz/⅓ cup) soft brown sugar
25 g (3 oz/⅓ cup) golden syrup
1 teaspoon baking powder
2 teaspoons ground ginger
½ teaspoon bicarbonate of soda
70 g (6 oz/1 ½ cups) icing sugar to decorate

Sieve the dry ingredients together. In another bowl, cream the margarine or butter, sugar and syrup until soft and light in texture. Work in the dry ingredients and knead the mixture thoroughly. Roll out the dough to a 6 mm (¼ in) thickness.

Make a template for the bear's head using a thin card. Dust the surface of the rolled out dough with a little flour, lay the template in position and carefully cut around the outside with a sharp knife. Repeat until all the dough is used.

Bake the biscuits on buttered baking sheets in the centre of a preheated oven at 210C (425F/ Gas 6-7) for 10 minutes.

When the biscuits are cool, pipe eyes, nose and mouth using the icing sugar blended with a little warm water to give a flowing consistency.

Makes 8-10 biscuits.

TEDDY BEAR CAKE

1 round sponge or fruit cake, either bought or homemade, about 20 cm (8 in) in diameter
Paste food colourings in pink, brown, blue, red, yellow, purple and green, or a selection of your choosing

MOULDING SUGAR PASTE:
3 small egg whites
2½ round tablespoons liquid glucose, slightly warmed
1.1 kg (2½ lb) icing sugar

To make the sugar paste, mix all the above ingredients together. Colour 450g (1lb) of the sugar paste pink. Wrap the rest of the sugar paste in plastic wrap until later.

Cover a cake board with a rolled out square of pink paste. Roll out more paste and cut four small rectangles for placemats. Place these aside to dry on baking parchment paper. Wrap up the remainder of the pink paste with plastic wrap.

Centre your cake on the board; if covered with marzipan, brush with a little water. If not, brush with warmed, sieved apricot jam. Roll out 450 g (1 lb) of white sugar paste to cover the cake, wrapping spare paste in plastic.

Drape the paste over the cake like a tablecloth. Gently push the folds of the paste into place, keeping your fingers dusted with icing sugar. Cut excess away with a sharp knife. Roll out five small shapes for plates. Adhere four of the plates to the placemats with a little water.

Make four differently-coloured crackers from pieces of paste. Colour some paste brown to make tiny buns. Top the buns with white paste and a little dot of red for a cherry. Place the buns on the fifth plate. Make a small parcel, with a ribbon and tiny flowers, from coloured paste.

Using four different colours, mould four bears. Each bear is basically the same shape. Make an oval piece for the body, two curved arms, two legs, a head and two ears. Create eyes and noses with the end of a cocktail stick.

Make stools from blue paste; leave to dry. Assemble the bears using a little water as glue and position them on the stools around the table.

GINGERBREAD HOUSES

6 teaspoons golden syrup

6 teaspoons black treacle (molasses)

30 g (1 oz/6 teaspoons) light soft brown sugar

60 g (2 oz/¼ cup) butter

185 g (6 oz/1½ cups) plain flour

1½ teaspoons ground ginger

½ teaspoon bicarbonate of soda

1 egg, beaten

DECORATION:

125 g (4 oz) white chocolate

125 g (4 oz) plain (dark) chocolate

pink, green and yellow food colourings

icing sugar for dusting

Preheat oven to 200C (400F/Gas 6). Line 2 baking sheets with non-stick baking paper. Put syrup, treacle (molasses), sugar and butter in a saucepan. Heat gently, stirring occasionally, until melted.

Sift flour and ginger into a bowl. Stir bicarbonate of soda into melted mixture, add to flour with enough beaten egg to mix to form a soft dough. Knead on a lightly floured surface until smooth and free from cracks. Cut off ⅓ dough; wrap in plastic wrap.

Roll out remaining ⅔ dough thinly and cut out thirty-two 4 cm (1½ in) squares of dough and place, spaced apart, on a baking sheet. Roll out remaining ⅓ dough and cut out sixteen 6 x 4 cm (2½ x 1½ in) oblongs. Cut an inverted 'V' at one of the short ends of each oblong to shape a 'pitch' for 'roof'. Each equal side should measure 2.5 cm (1 in).

Place on baking sheet and bake in the oven for 8-10 minutes until golden brown. Cool on wire rack.

Break up and place white and plain (dark) chocolate in separate bowls over hand-hot water. Stir occasionally until melted. Divide white chocolate between 3 small bowls and colour pink, green and yellow with food colourings.

Assemble each house using plain (dark) chocolate to stick 4 walls together, alternating 2 square and 2 'V' pieces. Then stick 2 other squares on top of structure to form 'pitched roof'. Leave to set. Spread remaining plain (dark) chocolate over non-stick baking paper.

When almost set, invert onto another piece of paper, peel off baking paper and cut chocolate into 2 cm (¾ in) squares for roof tiles. Secure tiles onto roof with melted chocolate, starting at base of each roof and working to top.

Using coloured chocolate, fill 3 greaseproof paper piping bags, snip off points and pipe in doors, windows and coloured beads down all the joins. Leave to set. Dust with icing sugar.

Makes 8.

MOBILES

155 g (5 oz/1¼ cups) plain flour
30 g (1 oz/9 teaspoons) custard powder
90 g (3 oz/⅓ cup) butter
45 g (1½ oz/8 teaspoons) caster sugar
1 egg white
6 teaspoons lemon juice
250 g (8 oz) clear fruit sweets
125 g (4 oz) white chocolate, melted
red and green oil-based, or powdered, food colourings
red and green ribbon

Preheat oven to 180C (350F/Gas 4). Line 2 baking sheets with non-stick baking paper. Sift flour and custard powder into a bowl.

Rub in butter finely. Stir in sugar, egg white and enough lemon juice to form a soft dough. Knead lightly; roll out to 0.5 cm (¼ in) thickness. Using a 5 cm (2 in) biscuit cutter, cut out 20 shapes; put on baking sheets, spaced apart.

Using a sharp knife or small cutters, cut out centres, leaving a 1 cm (½ in) frame. Make a hole at top of each. Put ½ a sweet into centres. Bake in the oven until sweets have melted. Cool on sheets.

Divide chocolate between 3 bowls. Colour one red and one green using food colourings. When chocolate has set enough to leave a trail on surface, fill 3 greaseproof paper piping bags with the mixtures, fold down tops and snip off points. Decorate biscuits with swirls, dots and lines of coloured chocolate.

When set, peel off paper, thread different lengths of ribbon through holes and hang up near the light so that the coloured centres shine.

Makes 20.

CARAMEL SHORTBREAD

SHORTBREAD
250 g (8 oz/2 cups) plain flour
pinch of salt
60 g (2 oz/¼ cup) caster sugar
185 g (6 oz/¾ cup) butter

CARAMEL:
125 g (4 oz/½ cup) unsalted butter
400 g (14.1 oz) can condensed milk
2 teaspoons instant coffee granules
60 g (2 oz/¼ cup) caster sugar
60 g (2 oz/2 tablespoons) golden syrup

TOPPING:
185 g (6 oz) plain (dark) chocolate, melted
30 g (1 oz) white chocolate, melted

Preheat oven to 180C (350F/Gas 4). To make shortbread, sift flour, salt and sugar into a bowl. Rub in butter until mixture forms coarse crumbs, then work together to form a soft dough. Roll out on a floured surface to an oblong a little smaller than a 32.5 x 22.5 cm (13 x 9 in) Swiss roll tin.

Place shortbread in tin; press out to fit. Prick all over with a fork. Chill for 30 minutes. Bake in the oven for 25-30 minutes until lightly browned. Cool.

To make caramel, in a heavy saucepan, stir ingredients over moderate heat until melted. Stirring, bring to a gentle boil; boil until mixture thickens and holds a trail, about 6-8 minutes.

Spread over shortbread. Cool. Spread plain chocolate over caramel. Put white chocolate into a paper piping bag, cut a small hole in bag; pipe lines across plain chocolate, 1 cm (½ in) apart. Pull a skewer through lines to decorate. Cut into squares when set.

Makes 48.

TOFFEE APPLES

CURD CHEESE POPETTES

450 g (1 lb/2¼ cups) sugar	
125 g (4 oz/½ cup) butter	
2 tablespoons white wine vinegar	
2 tablespoons boiling water	
red food colouring, if desired	
hot water	
8 medium-sized crisp apples, washed, dried, skewered from top with 8 wooden lollipop sticks or skewers	
iced water	

In a heavy-bottomed saucepan, combine sugar, butter, vinegar, boiling water and a few drops of red food colouring, if desired. Cook over low heat, stirring, until sugar is dissolved. Increase heat and boil, without stirring, until mixture reaches hard crack stage 147C (290F) on sugar thermometer or using a spoon, drop a little toffee into a small bowl of cold water to test.

Place saucepan in a larger saucepan of hot water to keep toffee soft. Quickly dip apples in toffee mixture, repeat for a thicker coating.

Dip coated apples into iced water to harden the toffee. Stand on greaseproof paper to cool. Wrap toffee apples in plastic wrap.

Makes 8 toffee apples.

90 g (3 oz/⅓ cup) butter	
155 g (5 oz/5¼ cups) crushed cornflakes	

FILLING:

375 g (12 oz) medium fat curd cheese	
155 ml (5 fl oz/⅔ cup) thick sour cream	
3 eggs, separated	
90 g (3 oz/⅓ cup) caster sugar	

TO DECORATE:

250 g (8 oz) small strawberries	

In a small saucepan, melt butter, then stir in crushed cornflakes. Mix well, then press mixture into 18 individual tartlet tins, dividing it equally between them.

In a bowl, beat cheese and sour cream until smooth. Add egg yolks and 60 g (2 oz/¼ cup) sugar and mix well.

Whisk egg whites in a separate bowl with remaining sugar until firm. Fold into cheese mixture with a large metal spoon.

Divide cheese mixture between moulds and decorate each with a strawberry.

Makes 18.

LEMONADE

MICKEY MOUSE

juice of 1 lemon
2 tablespoons sugar
cracked and cubed ice
water
spiral of lemon peel
slice of lemon

cola
ice cubes
1 scoop vanilla ice cream
whipped cream
2 maraschino cherries

Pour lemon juice and sugar over cracked ice in cocktail shaker. Mix well. Pour over cubed ice into glass. Fill with water. Stir. Garnish with spiral of lemon peel and slice of lemon and serve with a straw.

Pour cola over ice in tall glass. Add ice cream. Top with whipped cream and garnish with cherries. Serve with straws and a long-handled spoon.

PEACH COOLER

2 large peaches, skinned and stoned

juice of ½ lemon

two 150 g (5 oz) cartons peach yogurt

500 ml (16 fl oz/2 cups) milk

ice cubes

peach slices, to garnish

Put skinned peaches, lemon juice, yogurt and milk into a blender or food processor and process until completely smooth.

Fill tall glasses with ice cubes and pour over peach cooler. Garnish the sides of the glasses with thin slices of peach.

Serves 4-6.

SUNRISE & SUNSET

90 ml (3 fl oz/⅓ cup) apricot nectar juice

90 ml (3 fl oz/⅓ cup) pineapple juice

155 ml (5 fl oz/⅔ cup) sparkling lemonade

155 ml (5 fl oz/⅔ cup) sparkling orange juice

4 teaspoons grenadine syrup

crushed ice

2 lemon slices

2 cocktail umbrellas

2 drinking straws

Using 2 goblets or tumblers, pour apricot nectar into one glass and pineapple juice into another glass. Add lemonade to apricot juice and sparkling orange to pineapple juice.

Carefully spoon 2 teaspoons grenadine syrup into each drink, allowing it to settle at the bottom of each glass.

Add a little crushed ice, a lemon slice and a cocktail umbrella to each glass. Serve each with a drinking straw.

Makes 2.

SEASONAL PARTIES

Annual events such as Christmas and New Year's are perfect opportunities for celebrations, especially since they are national holidays. The recipes on the following pages are suitable for some of these more traditional party times but you do not have to be confined to these dates. Create a party around an event such as Midsummer's Night or a Saints Day such as St Patrick's Day.

THE CHRISTMAS HOLIDAY SEASON

Christmas is the most busy season for entertaining. Many people find their social diaries filling up quickly around November, so you must remember to prepare your party well in advance. Frequently, people hold two sorts of parties; one for their friends that takes place before or just after Christmas and one that is for their family on Christmas Day. Consider changing tradition and combining the two parties. Also, consider moving the dates around; you may find that it will benefit most people to attend a party or dinner that is held well before Christmas or during the week between Christmas and New Year's Day. This week is also a good opportunity to gather friends and neighbours for some mulled wine and Christmas cake (see pages 89-90 for suggestions).

For a Christmas dinner, turkey and goose are the most common main courses, but choose duck, pheasant, ham or a combination of these dishes for variety. If you decide on a turkey, experiment slightly with the accompaniments. In this chapter are two excellent and unusual stuffings: Apple & Walnut, and Cranberry Orange (see page 87).

HALLOWEEN & FIREWORKS

If you decide to have a celebration on a fireworks night such as Guy Fawkes Day, or on Halloween, you may find the recipes on pages 92 and 93 suitable for these outdoor occasions.

Dishes such as Barbecue Beans & Bacon and Corned Beef Hash (page 92) are easy to make in large quantities and ideal to eat beside a bonfire or while watching a display of fireworks. French Bread Pizza and Crunchy Potato Skins are not only easy to eat and easy to hold (a definite bonus for outside eating) but are meals in themselves. In addition to these food items, you may want to set up a small table outside and have sausages and hot dogs available for grilling over the bonfire.

OTHER ANNUAL EVENTS

Use some of your family customs and traditions, whether passed down through generations or newly discovered, to create a unique and special occasion for your family and close friends.

Or, create a menu around a little-celebrated holiday. For example, prepare a range of egg dishes for an Easter party (see pages 11, 14, and 45 for suggestions). Or serve heart-shaped food (see page 68) and tomato juice-based cocktails for Valentine's Day.

Whatever you choose, reflect the festive spirit of the occasion in the food and drink you serve. The following recipes and recipes in other chapters of this book are just the starting point for a party which could become an annual tradition in itself.

Above: Make a jolly lantern to put you in the Halloween 'spirit'. First cut the top off a pumpkin. Scoop out the inside to use later for a pumpkin pie. Now mark the eyes, nose and mouth with a black marker or pen and carefully cut these features out. Place a small candle inside, light, and put the pumpkin top back on.

Left: Christmas is a time to share with friends and family as well as to indulge in delicious food. Make the traditional turkey dinner extra special by garnishing with green and red decorations. Use cranberries, holly and mistletoe but ensure that no child attempts to eat the decorations by mistake.

ROAST STUFFED TURKEY

4 kg (8 lb) oven-ready turkey with giblets
250 g (8 oz/4¼ cups) soft
white breadcrumbs
1 large onion, finely chopped
3 sticks celery, finely chopped
finely grated peel and juice of 1 lemon
8 plums, chopped
155 ml (5 fl oz/⅔ cup) red wine
500 g (1 lb/2 cups) chestnut purée
3 teaspoons each of chopped fresh sage,
thyme and oregano
salt and pepper
500 g (1 lb) rashers fat streaky bacon
60 g (2 oz/½ cup) plain flour

Remove giblets from turkey, place in a saucepan with 625 ml (20 fl oz/ 2½ cups) water and bring to boil. Cover and simmer for 1 hour. Strain stock into a bowl; reserve liver.

In a saucepan, place breadcrumbs, onion, celery, lemon peel and juice, plums and wine. Bring to boil, while stirring, and cook for 1 minute.

Put chestnut purée, herbs, salt and pepper to taste and turkey liver into a food processor fitted with a metal blade. Process until smooth. Add breadcrumb mixture and process until evenly blended.

Place ⅓ stuffing into neck end of turkey, pull over flap of skin and secure under turkey with skewers or string. Fill cavity of turkey with remaining stuffing, pull skin over parson's nose and secure with skewers or string. Truss turkey with string, securing wings and legs closely to body, and place in a roasting tin.

Cover the whole turkey with rashers of streaky bacon to help keep it moist during cooking.

Preheat oven to 190C (375F/Gas 5). Cook turkey in the oven for 2 hours, remove from oven; remove bacon if you require it for serving, and cover turkey and tin with thick foil. Return to oven for a further 1- 1½ hours until turkey is tender and only clear juices run when pierced with a sharp pointed knife between legs of turkey.

Leave to stand in tin for 20 minutes before removing. Remove any skewers or trussing string and place turkey on a warmed serving dish. Chop crispy bacon finely.

To make gravy, blend flour and a little stock together in a pan until smooth. Pour remaining stock into roasting tin, stir well, strain gravy into saucepan with flour mixture. Bring to boil, stirring until thickened; cook for 2 minutes. Season to taste with salt and pepper and pour into a gravy boat.

Serve turkey with bread sauce, sausages, crisp bacon and gravy.

Serves 10.

GOOSEBERRY GOOSE

CRANBERRY & ORANGE DUCK

4 kg (8 lb) oven-ready goose, with giblets
12 rashers streaky bacon
3 teaspoons Dijon mustard
250 ml (8 fl oz/1 cup) elderflower wine
500 g (1 lb) gooseberries, cooked
3 teaspoons arrowroot
30 g (1 oz/5 teaspoons) caster sugar
50 g (2 oz) elderberries, if desired

STUFFING:

30 g (1 oz/6 teaspoons) butter
6 shallots, finely chopped
155 ml (5 fl oz/⅔ cup) gooseberry juice
30 g (1 oz/1¼ cups) chopped fresh mixed herbs
375 g (12 oz/6¼ cups) soft breadcrumbs
1 teaspoon salt
1 teaspoon ground black pepper

Preheat oven to 220C (425F/Gas 7). Remove giblets from goose; reserve liver. Use giblets to make stock. Prick goose skin all over.

To make stuffing, melt butter in a pan, add shallots and liver; fry for 2 minutes. Stir in ½ gooseberry juice, herbs, all but 6 teaspoons of breadcrumbs and salt and pepper.

Stuff neck end of goose; place remainder in body cavity. Cover goose with bacon; cook in oven for 45 minutes. Reduce oven to 190C (375F/Gas 5); cook for 1½ hours, pouring off excess fat during cooking.

Remove bacon, chop very finely; mix with remaining breadcrumbs. Brush goose with mustard; sprinkle with crumb mixture. Return to oven for a further 20-30 minutes until meat is tender.

Place on a serving plate. Pour away excess fat, add 60 ml (2 fl oz/¼ cup) stock to roasting tin, mix with remaining gooseberry juice, add wine, gooseberries, arrowroot and sugar. Boil for 1 minute, stirring. Process until smooth. Strain sauce and stir in elderberries, if desired.

Serves 6-8.

1 duck, about 2 kg (4 lb), cut into 4 joints
2 teaspoons arrowroot
2 teaspoons orange juice

MARINADE:

125 g (4 oz/1 cup) cranberries
8 teaspoons clear honey
2 teaspoons finely grated orange peel
6 teaspoons freshly squeezed orange juice
155 ml (5 fl oz/⅔ cup) rosé wine
4 teaspoons chopped fresh sage
½ teaspoon each salt and black pepper

GARNISH:

orange slices
4 teaspoons cranberries
fresh sage leaves

Trim off excess fat and skin from duck joints to neaten.

To make marinade, place cranberries and honey in a small saucepan with 155 ml (5 fl oz/⅔ cup) water and boil. Cover and cook for 3 or 4 minutes, until tender. Press through a sieve to purée. Stir in remaining marinade ingredients.

Add duck joints to marinade and turn to coat evenly. Cover with plastic wrap and leave in a cool place for 4 hours or overnight.

Preheat oven to 220C (425F/Gas 7). Remove duck joints from marinade and arrange in an ovenproof dish. Cook for 45 minutes. Reduce temperature to 190C (375F/Gas 5). Pour marinade over duck, cover and cook for 40 minutes, or until duck is cooked and juices run clear when pierced with tip of knife. Place on a serving plate and keep warm.

Blend arrowroot and orange juice in a small pan. Pour off most of fat from marinade, add marinade to arrowroot mixture. Bring to boil, stirring, then cook gently 1 minute, until thick and clear. Pour sauce over duck, then garnish.

Serves 4.

CRANBERRY ORANGE STUFFING

APPLE & WALNUT STUFFING

250 g (8 oz/2 cups) cranberries
finely grated peel and juice of 2 oranges
9 teaspoons clear honey
30 g (1 oz/6 teaspoons) butter
2 onions, chopped
1 teaspoon salt
½ teaspoon ground black pepper
½ teaspoon cayenne pepper
1 teaspoon ground mace
4 teaspoons chopped fresh sage
250 g (8 oz/4¼ cups) soft
white breadcrumbs
90 g (6 oz/½ cup) pine nuts

Place cranberries, orange peel and juice in a saucepan.

Bring to boil, cover and simmer very gently for 1 minute until just tender. Remove saucepan from heat. Stir in honey and pour cranberries into a bowl.

Melt butter in a saucepan, stir in onions and cook gently for 2 minutes until tender. Add salt, pepper, cayenne, mace and sage; mix until well blended.

Stir onion mixture into cranberries with breadcrumbs and pine nuts until well mixed.

Sufficient for a 4 kg (8 lb) turkey or goose. Halve the recipe for a duck.

30 g (1 oz/6 teaspoons) butter
4 shallots, chopped
500 g (1 lb) cooking apples, grated
finely grated peel and juice of 1 lemon
125 g (4 oz/2 cups) soft
white breadcrumbs
6 teaspoons chopped fresh thyme
½ teaspoon salt
½ teaspoon ground black pepper
60 g (2 oz/½ cup) chopped walnuts
5 pickled walnuts, sliced
1 egg, beaten

Melt butter in a saucepan, add shallots, apples, lemon peel and juice.

Cook over a moderate heat, stirring occasionally, until onion and apple are tender. Remove saucepan from heat. In a bowl, mix together breadcrumbs, thyme, salt, pepper and chopped and pickled walnuts.

Add apple mixture and beaten egg and stir well until evenly blended.

Sufficient for a 2.5-3 kg (5-6 lb) goose or duck. Double the recipe for a large turkey.

SOUFFLÉ POTATOES

ALMOND BRUSSEL SPROUTS

4 large potatoes
30 g (1 oz/6 teaspoons) butter
6 teaspoons single (light) cream
1 teaspoon salt
½ teaspoon ground black pepper
½ teaspoon grated nutmeg
2 eggs, separated

Preheat oven to 220C (425F/Gas 7). Scrub potato skins and remove any 'eyes'. Pierce each potato several times using a small, sharp knife, and arrange on a baking sheet. Cook in the oven for 1 hour, or until potatoes are tender.

Cut each potato in half, carefully scoop out the potato flesh and place in a bowl or an electric mixer fitted with a beater. Replace potato skins on a baking sheet and cook in the oven for 10-15 minutes until crisp and golden. Meanwhile mash or beat potato until smooth, add butter, cream, salt, pepper, nutmeg and egg yolks. Mash or beat until thoroughly blended.

Stiffly whisk egg whites, add to potato and fold in gently, using a spatula, until evenly mixed. Fill each potato skin with mixture and return to oven for 10-15 minutes or until risen and lightly browned. Serve immediately.

Serves 8.

Variations: Add 125 g (4 oz) chopped crispy bacon or grated cheese to filling for a change, or add chopped mixed herbs to taste.

500 g (1 lb) small Brussel sprouts
30 g (1 oz/6 teaspoons) butter
30 g (1 oz/¼ cup) flaked almonds
1 clove garlic, crushed
1 teaspoon finely grated lemon peel
1 teaspoon lemon juice
½ teaspoon salt
½ teaspoon ground black pepper
lemon twists and herb sprigs, to garnish

Trim stalks off sprouts and make a cut across each one. Cook in boiling, salted water for 4-5 minutes until just tender. Drain well and place in a warmed serving dish.

Meanwhile, melt butter in a small frying pan, add flaked almonds and garlic and fry until almonds are golden brown. Stir in lemon peel and juice and salt and pepper. Mix well.

Sprinkle almond mixture over sprouts and stir gently to mix. Serve immediately, garnished with lemon twists and herb sprigs.

Serves 4.

ROUND CHRISTMAS PUDDING

BRANDY BUTTER

500 g (1 lb/3 cups) mixed dried fruit	
60 g (2 oz/½ cup) chopped prunes	
45 g (1½ oz/⅓ cup) chopped glacé cherries	
60 g (2 oz/½ cup) chopped almonds	
45 g (1½ oz/¼ cup) grated carrot	
45 g (1½ oz/¼ cup) grated cooking apple	
finely grated peel and juice of 1 orange	
3 teaspoons black treacle (molasses)	
90 ml (3 fl oz/⅓ cup) stout	
3 teaspoons brandy plus extra for serving	
1 egg	
60 g (2 oz/¼ cup) butter, melted	
60 g (2 oz/⅓ cup) dark soft brown sugar	
¾ teaspoon ground allspice	
60 g (2 oz/½ cup) plain flour	
60 g (2 oz/1 cup) soft white breadcrumbs	

In a large mixing bowl, put mixed fruit, prunes, cherries, almonds, carrot, apple, orange peel and juice, treacle, stout and the brandy. Mix well together. Stir in egg, butter, sugar, allspice, flour and breadcrumbs until well blended.

Cover; leave in a cool place until ready to cook.

Use a buttered round Christmas pudding mould, measuring 12.5 cm (5 in) in diameter, or a rice steaming mould, lined with double thickness foil. Fill each half of mould with mixture. Place two halves together, securing mould.

Half-fill a saucepan with water, bring to the boil and place mould carefully into pan so that water comes just below join of mould. Cover and cook very gently for 6 hours. Cool in mould; turn out and wrap in foil until required.

To re-heat pudding: unwrap and replace in mould. Cook as before for 2-3 hours. Turn onto a serving plate, decorate with holly, spoon over warmed brandy and set alight. Serve with Brandy Butter, see opposite.

Serves 8.

185 g (6 oz/¾ cup) unsalted butter	
185 g (6 oz/¾ cup) caster sugar	
90 ml (3 fl oz/⅓ cup) brandy	

Put butter in a bowl or food processor fitted with a metal blade. Beat or process butter until white and creamy. Add sugar and beat or process until light and fluffy.

Add brandy, a drop at a time, beating continuously until enough has been added to well-flavour the butter. Take care the mix does not curdle through overbeating.

Pile butter into a glass dish and serve with a spoon, or, if preferred, spread the mixture about 1 cm (½ in) thick over a flat dish and leave to set hard. Using a fancy cutter, cut Brandy Butter into shapes and arrange in a serving dish.

Serves 8.

SOUTHERN COMFORT CAKE

TINY CHOCOLATE LOGS

315 g (10 oz/1¼ cups) butter
10 tablespoons golden syrup
315 ml (10 fl oz/1¼ cups) Southern Comfort
finely grated peel and juice of 1 orange
finely grated peel and juice of 1 lemon
1.15 kg (2¼ lb/6¼ cups) mixed dried fruit
315 g (10 oz/2½ cups) dried apricots, chopped
315 g (10 oz/2¼ cups) dried dates, chopped
¾ teaspoon bicarbonate of soda
3 eggs
500 g (1 lb/3½ cups) wholemeal self-raising flour
2 teaspoons ground allspice
125 ml (4 fl oz/½ cup) apricot jam
250 g (8 oz/2¼ cups) assorted nuts
apricots and dates, to decorate

Preheat oven to 150C (300F/Gas 2). Grease and double-line a 25 x 20 cm (10 x 8 in), 5 cm (2 in) deep, oblong tin with greaseproof paper. Place tin on a double-lined baking sheet.

In a large saucepan, place butter, golden syrup, Southern Comfort, orange and lemon peels and juices. Heat until almost boiling. Add mixed fruit, apricots and dates; stir until well blended and leave until almost cold. Add bicarbonate of soda, eggs, flour and allspice and stir until thoroughly mixed.

Spoon mixture into tin, level top; bake in the oven for 2¼-2½ hours or until a skewer inserted in the centre comes out clean. Cool in tin, then turn out and wrap in foil until required.

Boil and sieve apricot jam. Cut cake into 6 pieces, brush with apricot jam, arrange nuts and fruit over top; glaze with remaining jam. Leave until set, then wrap in plastic wrap and tie with ribbon.

Makes 6 individual cakes.

3 eggs
45 g (1½ oz/8 teaspoons) caster sugar
30 g (1 oz/¼ cup) plain flour
3 teaspoons cocoa

FILLING AND DECORATION:

315 ml (10 fl oz/1¼ cups) double (thick) cream
125 g (4 oz) plain (dark) chocolate
marzipan toadstools

Preheat oven to 200C (400F/Gas 6). Line a 30 cm (12 in) baking tray (with edges) with non-stick baking paper. Place eggs and sugar in a bowl over a saucepan of simmering water and whisk until thick and pale.

Remove bowl from saucepan, continue whisking until mixture leaves a trail when whisk is lifted. Sift flour and cocoa onto surface of mixture and fold in carefully until mixture is evenly blended. Pour mixture onto baking tray and spread out carefully to edges.

Bake in the oven for 8-10 minutes, or until firm to the touch. Cool slightly, turn out and remove paper, then trim edges and cut in half lengthwise.

Place 60 ml (2 fl oz/¼ cup) cream in a bowl with chocolate. Place over a pan of hot water; stir until melted. Whip remaining cream until almost thick.

When chocolate has cooled, fold it carefully into whipped cream. Using ⅓ chocolate cream, spread over each strip of sponge. Roll each into a firm roll from the long edge. Wrap in plastic wrap and chill until firm.

Cut each roll into 6 lengths, spread each with remaining chocolate cream, mark cream into lines. Decorate with marzipan toadstools. Keep the rolls cool until ready to serve.

Makes 12.

SCOTTISH BLACK BUN

315 g (10 oz) packet white bread mix
1 egg yolk
purple and green food colourings
FILLING:
250 g (8 oz/1 cup) mixed dried fruit
30 g (1 oz/¼ cup) chopped glacé cherries
30 g (1 oz/¼ cup) chopped flaked almonds
finely grated peel and juice of 1 orange
30 g (1 oz/6 teaspoons) light
soft brown sugar
60 g (2 oz/¼ cup) butter, melted
60 g (2 oz/½ cup) plain flour
1 teaspoon ground allspice
1 egg, beaten

Make up bread mix as directed on packet.

Knead for 5 minutes, place in a polythene bag and leave until filling has been made. Preheat oven to 180C (350F/Gas 4). Lightly flour 2 baking sheets.

To make filling, put dried fruit, cherries, almonds and orange peel and juice in a mixing bowl. Mix together with a wooden spoon. Add sugar, butter, flour, allspice and whole egg and stir well until all ingredients are evenly mixed.

Knead dough on a lightly floured surface and cut into 11 pieces. Roll out thinly, one piece at a time, to a 10 cm (4 in) round; reserve trimmings. Brush edge of round with water, place a heaped spoonful of filling in centre of dough.

Draw up edge of dough to cover filling, seal in centre and shape into a neat ball. Turn bun over with join underneath. Place on baking sheet. Repeat to make 10 in total. Prick buns all over with a fine skewer.

Roll out remaining dough very thinly; cut out 10 thistle shapes, stems and leaves. Brush each bun with 1 teaspoon of egg yolk mixed with a little water to glaze. Bake in the oven for 25 minutes, then remove from oven.

Divide remaining egg yolk in half, colour one half purple and one half green with food colourings. Brush thistles purple and leaves and stems green. Return to oven for a further 5 minutes until glaze has set and buns are golden brown. Cool on a wire rack.

Makes 10 buns.

BARBECUE BEANS & BACON

250 g (8 oz/1¼ cups) haricot beans, soaked overnight

30 g (1 oz/2 tablespoons) soft brown sugar

1 teaspoon salt

4 teaspoons black treacle

4 teaspoons red wine vinegar

2 teaspoons dry mustard

1 teaspoon Worcestershire sauce

pinch ground cinnamon

315 ml (10 fl oz/1¼ cups) tomato juice

2 large onions, chopped

500 g (1 lb) smoked gammon, cubed

chopped fresh chives, to garnish

crusty bread and butter, to serve

Drain beans and put in a large saucepan. Add enough water to cover the beans by 2.5 cm (1 in). Bring to the boil and boil rapidly for 15 minutes, then cover and simmer for 1 hour until the beans are tender. Meanwhile, heat the oven to 140C (275F/Gas 1).

Drain beans, reserving the water, and put in a casserole. Combine sugar, salt, treacle, vinegar, mustard, Worcestershire sauce, cinnamon and tomato juice and stir into the beans. Add onions and enough of the reserved water to just cover the beans. Cover the casserole and bake in the oven for 2 hours, checking occasionally to see if you need to add more water.

Stir in gammon, re-cover and cook the casserole for a further 1 hour. Garnish with chopped chives and serve each portion with plenty of crusty bread and butter.

Serves 6-8.

CORNED BEEF HASH

1 tablespoon vegetable oil

3 rashers smoked streaky bacon

1 onion, chopped

500 g (1 lb) potatoes, cooked and diced

340 g (10½ oz) can corned beef, diced

1 large egg, beaten

9 teaspoons single (light) cream

salt and pepper

2 tablespoons chopped fresh parsley

parsley sprigs and tomato slices, to garnish

Heat oil in a large frying pan. Remove rind from the bacon and chop the bacon finely. Add bacon and onion to the pan and cook for 2-3 minutes. Remove with a slotted spoon, leaving any oil in pan.

In a bowl, mix together bacon, onion, potatoes, corned beef, egg, cream, salt and pepper and parsley. Return to the pan and press down firmly. Cook over a medium heat for 15-20 minutes until well browned on the bottom.

Turn over and cook for a further 5-10 minutes. Garnish with sprigs of parsley and slices of tomato and serve at once.

Serves 4-6.

CRUNCHY POTATO SKINS

FRENCH BREAD PIZZA

6 medium floury potatoes
4 tablespoons cooking oil
6 rashers smoked streaky bacon
2 small avocado pears
1 clove garlic, crushed
2-3 teaspoons lemon juice
2-3 teaspoons Greek yogurt
2 drops Tabasco sauce
salt and pepper
fresh herb sprigs, to garnish

Preheat the oven to 200C (400F/ Gas 6). Scrub potatoes and prick them all over with a fork. Bake in the oven for 1 hour until just tender. Remove from the oven and turn up the heat to 220C (425F/Gas 7).

Pour oil into a shallow roasting dish and put into the oven to heat. Remove rind from the bacon and grill the bacon until crisp and golden. Drain well.

Peel and stone avocados and mash the flesh with garlic, lemon juice, yogurt, Tabasco sauce and salt and pepper. Cut potatoes in half lengthways. Using a teaspoon, scoop out most of the potato flesh, leaving a layer next to the skin. (Reserve the potato for making samosas or potato waffles.) Sprinkle skins with salt and put into the hot oil. Baste with oil, then turn hollow side up and bake in the oven for 25 minutes, basting regularly, until the potatoes are golden and crunchy.

Drain the potatoes on absorbent kitchen paper, then fill the cavities with avocado cream. Cut bacon into small strips and scatter over the potatoes. Garnish with fresh herbs and serve at once.

Serves 4-6.

1 medium French stick
4 tablespoons olive oil
440 g (14 oz) can tomatoes
salt and pepper
220 g (7 oz) can tuna fish in oil, drained
6-8 pimento-stuffed olives
60 g (2 oz/½ cup) grated Edam cheese
3 spring onions, chopped

TO SERVE:
green salad

Preheat oven to 180C (350F/Gas 4). Cut a slice from the top of French stick along whole length. Scoop out most of the soft crumb from base portion (this and the lid will not be required but can be used for breadcrumbs).

Brush inside of loaf with half the olive oil. Drain tomatoes and reserve juice. Brush inside of loaf with juice. Place loaf on a baking sheet and bake in the oven for 10 minutes.

Chop tomatoes and arrange half inside the loaf. Season to taste with salt and pepper. Flake tuna fish and spoon over tomatoes. Season again. Top with remaining tomatoes and season once again.

Halve olives and arrange on top. Sprinkle with grated cheese. Return to oven and bake for a further 15 minutes. Sprinkle with chopped spring onions and serve at once with salad.

Serves 2.

CHRISTMAS EVE MULL

1 bottle white wine
1 bottle red wine
315 ml (10 fl oz/1¼ cups) sweet red vermouth
3 teaspoons Angostura bitters
6 strips orange peel
8 whole cloves
1 cinnamon stick
8 cardamom pods, crushed
3 teaspoons raisins
125 g (4 oz/½ cup) caster sugar
lemon, lime, orange and apple slices, to decorate

Pour white and red wines into a stainless steel or enamel saucepan.

Add vermouth, bitters, orange peel, cloves, cinnamon and cardamom pods. Heat wine mixture gently until very hot, but do not boil. Remove saucepan from heat, cover with a lid and allow to cool. Strain wine into a bowl.

Just before serving, return wine to a clean saucepan, add raisins and sugar. Heat gently until sugar has dissolved and wine is hot enough to drink. Decorate with fruit slices and serve in heatproof glasses or mugs.

Serves 18.

HOT BUTTERED RUM

4 cinnamon sticks
4 teaspoons light soft brown sugar
125 ml (4 fl oz/½ cup) dark rum
625 ml (20 fl oz/2½ cups) cider
30 g (1 oz/6 teaspoons) butter
1 teaspoon ground mace
4 lemon slices

Divide cinnamon sticks, sugar and rum between 4 warm, heatproof glasses or mugs.

Place cider in a saucepan and heat until very hot, but not boiling. Fill each glass or mug almost to the top with cider.

Add a knob of butter, a sprinkling of mace and a lemon slice to each glass or mug. Stir well and serve hot.

Serves 4.

BUCK'S FIZZ

orange juice

1 dash Grenadine, if desired

chilled champagne

slice of lime

Fill glass one-third full with orange juice. Add Grenadine. Top with champagne. Garnish with a slice of lime.

KIR ROYALE

2 dashes crème de cassis

chilled champagne

Place crème de cassis in glass and fill with champagne.

INDEX

PICTURE CREDITS

The majority of the photographs in this book are the copyright of Salamander Books Ltd. Other copyrighted photographs are credited as follows on the page: (R) Right, (L) Left.

Anthony Blake: 6, 8(R)

Merehurst Press: 9, 10, 12, 13(R), 18, 19, 23(R), 31(R), 39, 40(R), 45(R), 46, 47, 48, 49, 50(L), 54, 55(R), 63(L), 73(R), 80(R), 81, 82, 93(R), 95